Awaken! A Guide to Becoming Conscious

By the Rev. Dr. Bob Ulbrich

Copyright © Bob Ulbrich 2015 All Rights Reserved

Contents

INTRODUCTION 1

PART 1 - TIME TO WAKE UP 4

Chapter 1- Your Alarm Clock is Going Off 5

Chapter 2 - The Rules 9

Chapter 3 - The Crystal 11

Chapter 4 - Don't Believe Everything You Think
.... 20

Chapter 5 - It Is Time for a New Religion 24

Chapter 6 - Religions 31

Chapter 7 - Hear the Symphony 35

Chapter 8 - The Next Stage of Evolution 39

PART 2 - WAKING IN THE DREAM 46

Chapter 9 - What is Consciousness? 47

Chapter 10 - Ancient History and Its Effect on Today's Culture 49

Chapter 11 - Relationships 57

Chapter 12 - Wounding Through the Ages 62

Chapter 13 - Who Are You, Really? 74

Chapter 14 - The Rainbow Perspective 79

Chapter 15 - Who Will Do the Driving? 82

Chapter 16 - Moiré Patterns and Reality 85

Chapter 17 - The Pattern and the Interpretation .90

Chapter 18 - Moiré Patterns and Time 96

Chapter 19 - The Nature of Evil 98

Chapter 20 - Heaven and Hell 100

Chapter 21 - Waking in the Dream 102

Chapter 22 - Getting To Know Yourself 106

Chapter 23 - Ecstatic Dance 110

Chapter 24 - Meditation.................................125

Chapter 25 - Getting Into Your Observer State 140

Chapter 26 - An Example of Healing From the Observer State 147

Chapter 27 - Chemical Means of Exploring Consciousness 151

PART 3 - WAKING FROM THE DREAM 172

Chapter 28 - Freedom 173

Chapter 29 - Attitude 176

Chapter 30 – How to Change Reality 181

Chapter 31 - Non-Newtonian Fluids as a Model of the Quantum Flux and the Creation of Reality Via Observation 187

Chapter 32 - The Shape of Time 190

Chapter 33 - The Causal Nexus 195

Chapter 34 - Ripples of Consciousness 200

Chapter 35 - Holograms, Fractals and Reality .202

Chapter 36 - Fractal Reality 210

Chapter 37 - Life as a Fractal Zoom 217

Chapter 38 - Filling in the Gaps 223

Chapter 39 - Being Present With Immortality ..232

Chapter 40 - Your Alarm Clock Is Going Off ..237

ABOUT THE AUTHOR..**243**

Introduction

"You live like this, sheltered, in a delicate world, and you believe you are living. Then you read a book... or you take a trip... and you discover that you are not living, that you are hibernating. The symptoms of hibernating are easily detectable: first, restlessness. The second symptom (when hibernating becomes dangerous and might degenerate into death): absence of pleasure. That is all. It appears like an innocuous illness. Monotony, boredom, death. Millions live like this (or die like this) without knowing it. They work in offices. They drive a car. They picnic with their families. They raise children. And then some shock treatment takes place, a person, a book, a song, and it awakens them and saves them from death. Some never awaken."

— Anaïs Nin, *The Diary of Anaïs Nin, Vol. 1: 1931-1934*

"We are here to awaken from our illusion of separateness." — Thich Nhat Hanh

There is a shift happening around the world. More and more people are waking up, realizing they have been operating as if in a trance and are now becoming conscious. At first glance, they look just like everyone else. They work and drive and picnic with their families and raise their children. But there is something different about them; they are different from their co-workers, different from their families, different from who they were before. They are on a new path, co-creating a new paradigm. Shift happens. And once it does, once you are on that path, there is no turning back.

There are ways to recognize these conscious awakened people. For one thing, they tend to not get caught up in the way things "should" be, tend not to judge others for not conforming to social norms, and tend to respect the paths others are on while they themselves follow their own path without concern for whether or not it is the socially acceptable path. They also tend to be able to observe their mental states without getting caught up in that state; they don't believe everything they think. They have a tendency to respond rather than react; their intention is to choose their actions and reactions from a place of conscious evaluation rather than out of habit or reflex.

Conscious people also tend to be more empathetic and have a natural aversion to self-gain at the expense of others. And they tend to not act out subconsciously - this is essentially the definition of conscious behavior. They aspire to not suppress and repress issues and desires, only to have those issues and desires later bubble back up to the surface in unhealthy or manipulative ways. Rather, they bring these things into consciousness where they can then choose whether and how to act on them.

Something woke these people up. Maybe it was a chance meeting with an influential person. Maybe it was a participation in a transformative festival. Maybe it was a psychedelic drug experience. Maybe it was an ayahuasca shamanic ceremony. Maybe it was a book. Maybe it will be this book.

Part 1 - Time to Wake Up

Chapter 1- Your Alarm Clock is Going Off

Imagine for a moment a race a pan-dimensional hyper-beings whose job (insofar as beings such as these have jobs) is to examine all the myriad ways that the Multiverse can potentially be experienced. Powerful in ways we can't begin to imagine, these beings, were they to be seen from a human perspective, would appear as gods and goddesses; in fact, a human perspective might even seem recognize them and would call them with names such as Shiva, Zeus, Gaia, Loki.

Picture them hovering above a pool, or more accurately perhaps sitting in a pool much like you and I might sit with some friends in a hot tub. This hot tub, however, is not filled with water; it is instead filled with a strange liquid of potentialities, each molecule of which representing an entire potential alternate universe.

As they sit there gazing into the liquid, noting one molecule after another, Zeus points out a lone molecule and remarks how interesting this particular alternative universe is. Then Gaia notes how poignant another such alterative universe is. Suddenly Shiva gasps as he notices an extraordinarily brilliant universe, and the beings examine it with great interest. However, these beings do not merely observe potential realities but actually experience them from the inside.

These gods and goddesses can pick out a particular person in a particular universe, and experience that universe through their eyes, as easily as you or I might pick up a book and "experience" the story through the eyes of the protagonist. Even more easily, in fact, as these beings are outside of Time, and thus are able to experience an entire life, thousands of entire lifetimes, thousands of different versions of the same lifetime, without tiring or aging. The beings decide that this indeed is a universe worth experiencing. But then Shiva suggests that, just for kicks, they should all completely forget who they really are and where they come from. Instead, they should choose one reality to experience and forget all others.

They all decide to dive into this universe and experience it as human beings, and they must somehow all find each other without knowing their True Form. The years they choose to experience are during a particularly interesting phase of history. It is the time that paves the way to humanity's paradigm shift to a higher state of consciousness. Their job is to assist in this shift.

But while in human form they are unaware of the job that they have agreed to do because they have agreed to forget who they are and where they came from. By waking up to who they really are in the midst of experiencing their humanity, they infuse their consciousness and the pathway to awakening into the collective consciousness and affect all.

The beings set things up ahead of time so that "random chance" would lead them together, but recognizing each other when that happens will be the challenge they must meet. They also placed clues in the pathway of the lives they chose to experience.

The clues might take the form of books or movies, famous philosophical and religious writings, psychedelic experiences, "random" conversations, dreams. These clues were meant to help nudge them towards the Truth of who they really were and what Reality is really like. And then finally, after all the groundwork had been laid, they would find the final clue, the one that would act as a sort of alarm clock and put it all together for them, helping them to awaken to the Truth just at the optimal moment when the world really needed that hundredth monkey to awaken and tip the balance toward an enlightened humanity.

Imagine that that alarm clock is this book, that that luminous being having a human experience is you, and that you suddenly realize who you are and the true nature of Reality the moment you read this very sentence.

Still human and trapped in the Dream? Oh well, it was worth a try, but it looks as though we'll have to do it the hard way, that is, read to the end of the book.

Chapter 2 - The Rules

Humanity is shifting from a time of "following the rules" to a time of each individual looking within and following their own authentic path. The last 3 Ages (Taurus, Aries, and Pisces, spanning over 6000 years) has been about following the rules, laws laid down from Authority that must be followed. Now we are entering the Age of Aquarius, and we are emerging into a new paradigm. No longer will it be about following someone else's rules; instead, we will look within to find our own authentic path.

Each individual must learn to know themselves and find what is right and wrong for them, which is a very individual path and therefore cannot be extended to or imposed upon anybody else. This is a harder path, for it requires being Conscious, requires doing The Work. It's much easier to just follow a set of rules and not have to think about it beyond that, but that is humanity's childhood path, and it is now time to grow up and take responsibility for ourselves. This is why it is so important to awaken, to become conscious at this particular point in our history.

Ecstatic dance is one good tool for developing this skill - there are no rules, no steps to learn, you practice just having your own authentic dance in a non-judgmental environment and not worrying about what it looks like (see chapter 23).

Not following anybody's rules but our own does not mean that anything goes or that we can do anything we want without any thought as to consequences; it's still important to act with right action, to follow the path with heart. If it's not clear to you what that path looks like, perhaps you still need The Rules. My guess, though, is that if you are reading this book and are on the path to waking up, you no longer need The Rules.

Chapter 3 - The Crystal

We are all facets of a vast crystal, each reflecting an aspect of the divine. Each culture on this planet is a facet of a giant crystal; the entire crystal is humanity, and no facet is any more important to the whole than any other. Each religion is a facet of a crystal. The entire crystal is true spirituality.

Our consciousness is only one facet of the crystal while the other facets are all the parts of our subconscious. Our whole self is the entire crystal. Each way of looking at the world is like a single facet on a crystal; Truth is seen when the entire crystal is viewed.

A plane is defined mathematically by an equation with the general form aX+bY+cZ+d=0. For example, a particular plane defined by the particular equation X+2Y+3Z=0 is shown in the figure below.

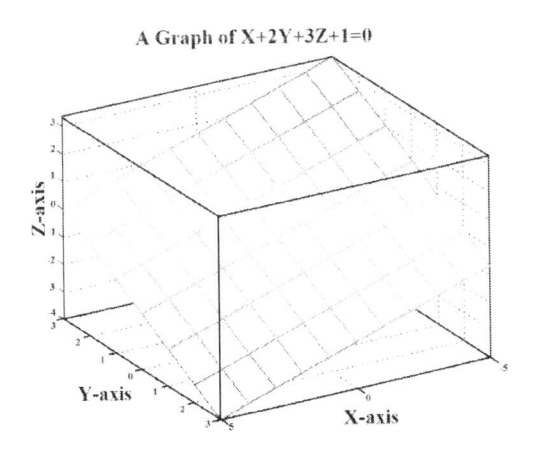

A Graph of X+2Y+3Z+1=0

Imagine, however, that you were to graph out equations that define concepts rather than mathematical correlations. Each axis now represents a different parameter by which to measure various concepts. If a particular equation produced a plane on the graph, that plane would represent one example of that concept, and every point on that plane would now represent a separate notion that fits within that example, while every point not on that plane would represent a notion that either has no bearing or is antithetical to the example.

For instance, if you were to take all the notions that fall under the category of the concept "Ways of Looking at the World" and place them all as separate points on a 3 dimensional graph, you might find that all the notions that have anything to do with, say, Religion would all be represented by points making up a specific plane. The equation for this plane would be the equation that defines the example of "Religion" in the general concept of "Ways of Looking at the World", for a religious outlook is one example of a way of looking at the world.

Another way of looking at the world is the scientific perspective, and all the notions with a scientific perspective would be represented by other points which would end up defining a different plane. Most of the points on the religious plane would fall well outside the scientific plane and vice versa, as there is little overlap in the two ways of looking at the world.

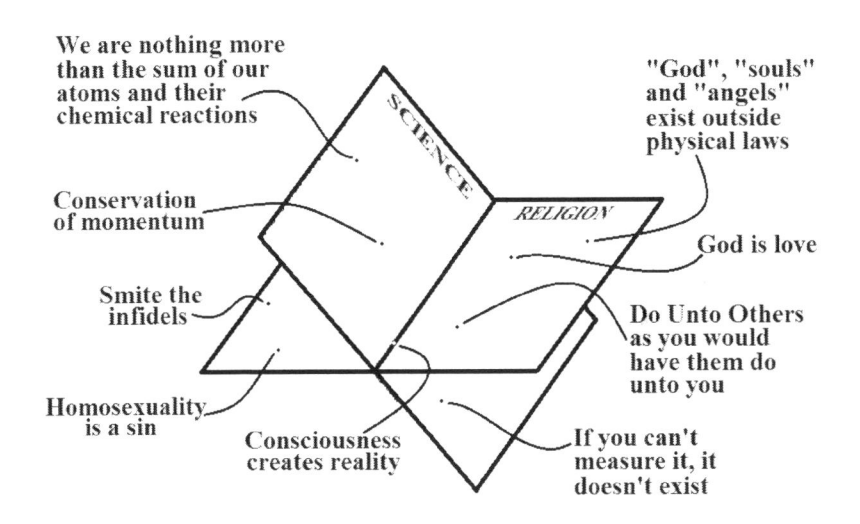

```
We are nothing more
than the sum of our                          "God", "souls"
atoms and their                              and "angels"
chemical reactions          SCIENCE          exist outside
                                             physical laws

Conservation
of momentum           RELIGION
                                             God is love

Smite the
infidels                                     Do Unto Others
                                             as you would
                                             have them do
                                             unto you
Homosexuality
is a sin         Consciousness               If you can't
                 creates reality             measure it, it
                                             doesn't exist
```

There are some points, though that fit with both Science and Religion. For example, the Indian Vedic philosophical tradition called Vedanta holds that consciousness is everything, and manifests, or creates, reality. This is precisely the conclusion that is drawn from experiments in quantum physics (see chapter 30). So here is a notion that fits on both the plane of Religion and the plane of Science, and its point would lie on the line where the two planes intersect.

Other equations define still other ways of looking at the world, perhaps for example from an astrological perspective. Again, there may be very little overlap with the religious or scientific perspectives, but there are some. For example, there is quite a lot of astrological imagery in the Bible.

One example of this is Moses' anger at his people for worshiping a golden calf (representing the past age, the age of Taurus) and not moving on to the new paradigm brought forth by the (then) new age of Aries (the ram, represented by sacrificial lambs, etc.), or of Jesus' feeding the multitude with two fishes, choosing fishermen as his disciples, and the fish symbol of Christianity as representing the (then) new age of Pisces and a (then) new paradigm (see chapter 12). So notions about biblical references to astrological ages would line on the line of intersection of the religious and astrological planes.

People who tend to look at the world in a religious way tend to see more of the notion-points on the religious plane as being "true", while people who tend to look at the world in a scientific way tend to see more of the notion-points on the scientific plane as being true. The truly true notion-points, the Universal Truths, tend to cluster in the center, while lesser truths tend to be more on the fringe. These may appear to be true, being in the same plane, and in fact are often vigorously defended as Absolute Truth by some who are exceptionally enthusiastic about viewing the world through that particular plane, but are actually just presumptions of truth that lie beyond the limits of usefulness of the system in question.

For example, consider the plane that represents religion. In the center are the dots that represent concepts such as "be nice to each other" and "God is love". Far beyond this central area are the dots that might look valid from within the plane, but whose validity is inconsistent with greater Truths and must be questioned. These represent concepts such as "our religion is the only true religion" and "smite thy enemies in the Name of the Lord" and "homosexuality is a sin".

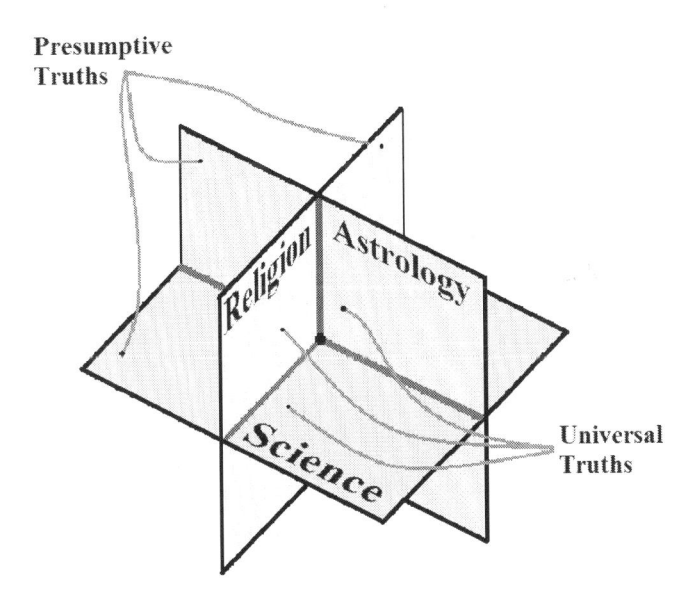

Presumptive Truths

Religion *Astrology*

Science

Universal Truths

If we eliminate all the questionable fringe points, trimming away the outlying perceived truths, we are left with just the sections of the planes that represent

Universal Truths, and the portions of the planes beyond the intersections, representing perceived truths, get erased. The remaining sections still contain points that overlap with each other, so that the sections still connect forming corners and vertices.

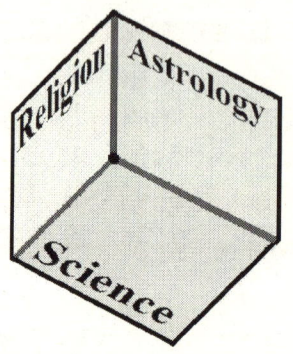

There are still other ways of looking at the world, defined by their own planes. Some of these planes don't intersect other planes at all; these two ways of viewing the world seem to be utterly incompatible no matter how you look, if you remain limited to two-dimensional thought.

But these two mutually exclusive planes are still connected to each other through yet other planes that intersect both of the first two. Now there is a link between two incompatible concepts that couldn't be perceived before. That link could never have been perceived without raising perception from 2 to 3 dimensions.

If we keep adding new planes of perception, each representing yet another way of looking at the world, and each time trim away the outlying perceived truths while keeping the universal truths, we will eventually be left with a complete 3-dimensional structure, much like a crystal, each facet of which represents the core universal truths of that particular way of looking at the world.

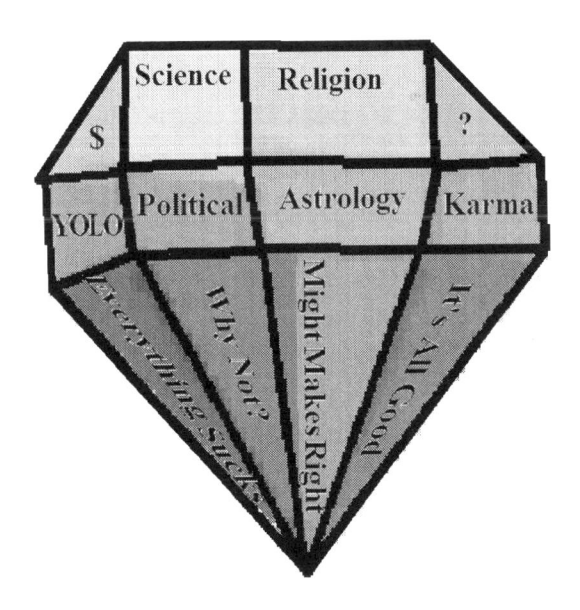

Of course, the crystal could represent many things besides "ways of looking at the world". The crystal could represent spirituality while each facet represents the core universal truths of each religion (see chapters 6 and 7). Or the crystal could represent any other complex system or concept that is made up of incongruent or disparate sub-units.

When we limit our thinking to two dimensions, we can only perceive one plane at a time, and other planes of thought appear to be blatantly ridiculous, such as the astrological plane from the perspective of the scientific plane. But if we can raise our perspective to higher dimensions, dimensions that can hold multiple planes at the same time, then we can perceive higher Truths that could not be perceived from our earlier limited perspective.

The Truth of all systems must be recognized and retained, the false extensions discarded, and the various systems linked together where they overlap. This allows us to see that most of the Truths of any one system can only be understood from the plane of thought of that system; they don't necessarily make any sense viewed from a different angle.

Holding all these Truths at once and seeing them from a higher three dimensional perspective allows seemingly mutually inconsistent Truths to become consistent with each other. From this perspective the entirety can be perceived. And from this perspective, the beauty of the entire crystal is revealed.

Chapter 4 - Don't Believe Everything You Think

Statements, facts, or concepts can be "true" to varying degrees along a spectrum, from the highly suspect ("it could theoretically be true, but really, what are the chances?") to the likely to be true ("there's a few special cases where that doesn't hold up, but generally this is the way things are") to the inherently true.

The inherently true would include statements that logicians call tautologies. Webster defines tautology as "necessarily true by virtue of the meaning of its component terms alone, without reference to external fact, and with its denial resulting in contradictions". An example would be "today is either Tuesday or some other day of the week". It seems clear that such a statement could never be false.

But it may be worth examining this. In order for the statement "today is either Tuesday or some other day of the week" to be false, one or more of the following two statements would have to be true: 1. "today is neither Tuesday nor another day of the week" or 2. "today is both Tuesday and another day of the week". Finding a true example of either of those statements throws the whole tautology assumption into question.

The first alternate statement can be true if you broaden your perspective to include other calendars. The Mayan Long Count calendar, for example, starts with 20 kin, or days, making 1 uinal, or 20-day period, while 18 uinals make a tun (a 360-day year). The uinal could be considered a Mayan week, but "Imix" in that week is neither Tuesday nor any other day of the week in the Gregorian calendar. So from the Mayan perspective the first alternate statement can indeed be true.

The second alternate statement can also be true if you broaden your perspective to include other parts of the world. It may be Tuesday just before midnight in this particular time zone, but just a few feet over there may be in an entirely different time zone in which it is Wednesday. So broadening your perspective can result in holding the truth that today is both Tuesday and another day of the week, and again the tautology is called into question.

So we see how when we hold something to be self-evidently true, that it may be worthwhile broadening our perspectives to include counter-intuitive examples as well, because Truth is rarely so cut and dry.

Changing our perspective also helps us not believe everything we feel when we get triggered about something. When something triggers us, we get caught up in a neutral network, a fragment of our whole self that expands and becomes our entire experience (see chapter 24), which includes associated feelings. Those feelings color the experience in such a way as to keep us trapped in that neural network.

You can tell when someone is emotionally triggered because their reaction is out of proportion to what the actual situation calls for. Triggers stem from old emotional wounds. Our brains are very good at associating new stimuli with old memories or old stories that persist even when the memories of what originally wrote that story have faded. A simple odor can bring back detailed memories of events that happened long ago. And emotionally charged situations can trigger deep feelings linked to similar situations from our past.

On the surface the triggered person seems to be reacting to the present situation, but the intensity of the reaction shows that on a subconscious level they are responding more to a situation that happened long ago. And sometimes our perceptions are distorted by "truths" that are both inaccurate and so deeply ingrained that they are never seen and therefore never questioned. These are "transparent beliefs" that are so "obvious" that we seldom stop to think that the situation could be any other way.

Transparent beliefs can trigger us into seeing a situation as being much more threatening than it really is, that can make a ditch look like a yawning chasm, too deep and scary to step into. Question the transparent beliefs that make the chasms look so deep and scary. Challenging that belief is both what makes taking that first step possible, and is the treasure waiting at the bottom of the "chasm".

When we recognize that we have been triggered, it helps to take a moment to pull back, not dive into the story that is before us, and mindfully examine the feelings that are coming up for us. Don't believe everything you feel!

From the higher perspective of our observer state (see chapter 25), we can critically examine those feelings and ask if they are really appropriate to the present situation. If they're not, don't believe them! A broader perspective changes everything.

We place a lot of value on our feelings. We go with our gut. If something feels true, we tend to believe it's true. But the Truth of our feelings is less true than tautologies, and we have seen that even tautologies are not always true.

So when you're triggered, broaden your perspective and see if it still feels the same from that higher level. If it doesn't feel the same, you may want to re-think what you're feeling, and re-feel what you're thinking.

Chapter 5 - It Is Time for a New Religion

We are now entering the Age of Aquarius, and with this New Age comes a new paradigm that requires consciousness. This new paradigm will cause a shift in the way we think about many things, including our relationship with Spirit. It is time to graduate to the next level of spirituality.

The cross has dominated as a symbol of the major spiritual paradigm, at least in Western culture, during the last age of Pisces. The cross represents the four directions, in two dimensions, of East-West and North-South. The ancient Earth-based religions honored the spirits of the four traditional directions in their ceremonies, associating them with various attributes.

East has been associated with the dawn, new beginnings, the element of air, the color yellow, and the ability to Know. I also associate East with the rhythm of lyrical (from the 5 rhythms work of Gabriel Roth, see chapter 23).

South has been associated with love and passion and transformation, the element of fire, the color red, and the quality of Will. I also associate it with the rhythm of staccato.

West has been associated with closures and completions, the element of water, the color blue, and Daringness. I also associate West with the rhythm of flow.

North has been associated with grounding and nurturing, the element of earth, the color green, the Mystery, and the ability to know when to keep silent. I also associate North with the rhythm of chaos.

The Wiccans add a fifth element of Spirit to the four elements of Earth, Air, Fire and Water, which is a step in the right direction, but they still have kept to two dimensions when they represent the five elements in their five-pointed pentagram.

I believe it is time to expand this into a full three dimensions by adding two new directions. The direction of Up I associate with Spirit, our higher selves, our wisdom and guidance, the element of ether, the color silver, and the rhythm of stillness.

The direction of Down I associate with our shadow, our subconscious, our creation of reality, the element of the quantum flux, the color black, and the synthesis of the five rhythms.

It is time for a new spiritual paradigm. I would not call it a new religion because religion to me refers to the codification people do to spiritual insights, and codifying my insights into rules of right and wrong behavior totally misses the point of what I believe (see chapter 6). It's not about what one should or should not do; it's about finding one's authentic path.

If you need a set of rules or commandments in order to know how to behave, if you can't find the answer within yourself as to what is right and wrong, then perhaps you need the old style of religion to guide you and you may not be ready to graduate to the new paradigm (see chapter 2). The higher truth is that there is no set of actions that are inherently "sinful"; it all depends on one's attitude with which one does the action.

Killing someone, for example, is generally considered "wrong" or "sinful" behavior, and it usually is because most people who would do such a thing do it out of anger or hatred or greed. But killing another person out of love and compassion, as for example euthanizing a terminally ill person who no longer wishes to live in constant pain, is not "wrong" or "sinful".

Likewise, helping the needy, but only in order to get that tax deduction, will not get you any closer to heaven. This is what Jesus meant when he said that if you commit the sin in your heart it is as bad as if you actually committed the sin with your actions. It's about the attitude, not the action.

If we are following the path that is authentic for ourselves, we will automatically act in accordance with Spirit. That authentic path will look different for each individual; no one can say what is right or wrong for another. We are all facets of a vast crystal, each reflecting an aspect of the divine (see chapter 3).

My facet has a different angle and reflects a different aspect of the divine from everyone else's facet, and every angle is equally important to the entire crystal. This is what the Bible means when it says to judge not, and to take the log out of your own eye before worrying about the speck in someone else's eye. We can only say what is right or wrong, what is authentic, for ourselves and not for anybody else.

How do we know what is authentic for ourselves? This is where doing The Work comes in. Getting to know ourselves, our organic self, shining the light into and transforming our shadow, is vitally important to the health of our souls and eliminating evil in the reality of our own personal universes. (For the purposes of this book, I am defining evil as self-gain at the expense of others, and the actions that result from this.) This is not easy work, but it is why we are here.

Our (personal) universes are created out of the quantum flux by our observing them to be, and our ability to observe them is there because they resonate with some aspect of our shadow - otherwise we wouldn't be able to see them. Again, using the crystal analogy from chapter 3, our conscious awareness is only one facet of a crystal; the other facets are all those parts of our subconscious, all those "hidden" (from our conscious selves) wounded and separated shadow parts of ourselves that often get triggered and rise to the surface to take over for a while, and then settle back into the muck leaving us to wonder why we reacted that way.

These other facets often make themselves known in the world around us. We couldn't recognize the things we experience in the world around us if there wasn't something deep within us that resonated with that part of the outside world. These deep parts of our subconscious therefore act as filters, letting through to our awareness those parts of the multiverse that resonate with some deep part of ourselves, allowing us to recognize it.

Therefore everything we experience in the world around us is reflected in some facet of the crystal within us. Our personal universe will continue to create situations that provide opportunities for us to deal with our shadow; if we don't deal with it the first time it will keep coming at us until we finally learn the lesson.

We can tell what it is we need to work on because it generally is at our boundary: the one place we feel we cannot go is the place we must. Boundaries are just walls we put around our issues. Do The Work. Shine a light into the shadow. Deal with the issues, and the need for boundaries goes away.

It generally looks scarier than it really is – go where you fear to go and fear will go. And you might as well; you will eventually have to deal with it within yourself or the Universe will make you deal with it in the world around you.

The Ages of Taurus, Aries and Pisces were about God-from-above (before the Age of Taurus, God, or rather the Goddess, was from below, associated with the Earth – see chapter 12). The Age of Aquarius is about God-from-within; the pathway to enlightenment is found doing the inner work.

The Work can utilize any number of different tools. Meditation (see chapter 24), ecstatic dance (see chapter 23), personal growth work, psychotherapy, Avatar training, Heart of Now, Lovetribe boundary exercises, Authentic Movement, Inner Yaga, Marshal Arts, Tantra, Shamanism, and psychedelics (see chapter 27) are just some of the potentially useful tools; it is up to the individual to find the best set of tools for their specific needs.

The new religion is all the religions. No more fighting over who has the better imaginary friend. Each religion is a facet of the crystal; God (or The Goddess or The Mystery or Spirit or whatever you want to call Him/Her/It) is the whole crystal. Every culture is a facet; humanity is the Crystal. Each of us is a facet; the crystal is the way the Universe is able to observe itself. It is time to honor everyone's perspective as a unique reflection of the divine.

Chapter 6 - Religions

I want to take a moment here to explain my view of religions and what you might call God. First of all, "God", by definition, is infinite, and therefore cannot be contained by anything, even a word. Anything that is named is reduced to the definition of that name, and the infinite cannot be reduced.

Using the word "God" automatically paints a picture in our heads of, for most of us, a male father-figure, and doesn't allow for all the infinite other aspects of Spirit. Take the gender aspect, for example. If God is infinite, God must be unique. But a "he" implies the possibility of a "she", an "other" that cannot exist if uniqueness is to be maintained; you can't have a gender if there is only one of you. I therefore feel more comfortable referring to "Spirit", or "The Universe" or "The Mystery", or "Source" rather than using the word "God" or one of His/Her myriad other names (even though these are also words that limit to their definition, but they are more vaguely defined and therefore less limiting).

I consider myself to be a spiritual person but I generally object to most religions. This is because religions tend to insist that their name for Spirit is the only acceptable True Name. I may be critical of religions, but not of the Truths those religions are based on.

Religion is what humans make of the Truths, and since humans are flawed, religions are flawed, but the Truths they are based on remain valid. All religions start with a download from Spirit to an individual who then becomes enlightened. The enlightened individual then tries to pass on this knowledge to others, but it is like trying to explain color to someone who has been blind all their life – much is lost in the translation and can never really be understood.

Those who hear the message can at least get a glimmer of enlightenment, but then they try to codify it into rules of acceptable and unacceptable behavior, and then others use the codes and rules to gain power and control over others, and finally you end up with a religion. But it is the original download, and only the original download, that is the important thing, not the religion that springs from it.

When I say that I am spiritual but not religious, I mean that I abide by the Truths that religions are based on, but do not follow the flawed rules and power structures of the religions themselves.

For example, an enlightened individual has their consciousness raised and realizes a sense of unity with all living things. Others can see the change in the enlightened one, and ask what it means to be in such a state. The enlightened one explains that in such a state one wouldn't do things like killing, lying, stealing, etc., because it just naturally wouldn't even occur to kill or steal from or lie to someone they felt a sense of unity with. They go on to say that in fact one way to recognize whether or not someone is indeed enlightened is by observing that they behave in this way. The people hearing this then say "oh, I get it, thou shalt not kill, thou shalt not steal, thou shalt not lie, and if we do these things we'll be enlightened." But they got it backwards.

Those behaviors aren't good or bad or right or wrong; there may be times or situations when any one of those behaviors may actually be appropriate. They are simply examples of how enlightened individuals generally do or don't act.

Religions, though, turn them into codes of behavior, if you do such and such you are sinning and therefore damned, and this is totally backwards from the original Message, and very judgmental. I reject all religions as flawed interpretations of the Truth and a means of controlling the masses.

I do, however, embrace the core Truths of all religions; I just reject what humans have done to these core Truths. It's people like Pat Robertson I object to when he claims that God sent the recent earthquake to the Haitians because their ancestors "made a deal with the devil" hundreds of years ago.

In this example it's not Christianity itself I object to, but only the religion of Christianity, and most of its leaders.

Chapter 7 - Hear the Symphony

I have often been judged by Christians as damned because many of my beliefs incorporate ideas that don't stem from Christianity. To be fair, I'm sure that if I lived in a predominantly Muslim country or any other religion it would be the same, it's just that it is Christians who I have the most contact with. I have a unique way of viewing things that doesn't fit into any one religion. This probably stems from my knack for seeing how disparate things fit together and seeing the whole puzzle by looking at a few pieces.

I also have had a tendency throughout my life to withhold judgment about people or ideas which has allowed me to see the good in people or the truth in ideas without having my vision distorted by preconceived notions. I can even hold two mutually incompatible ideas in my head at the same time, and keep doing so while discovering more pieces to the puzzle that fit in between, until things become connected in such a way that the two original ideas become no longer incompatible (see chapter 3).

When this happens I can see a glimpse of the Big Picture, can see how everything fits together in a huge multidimensional hyper-puzzle of amazing beauty and complexity. There are many pathways to Truth. My pathway looks different from everybody else's, since nobody else has my unique perspective and sees the universe the same way I do.

One example: the Christian concept of "Thy will be done", part of The Lord's Prayer, doesn't sit well with me because to me it feels like it has an undertone of "well I REALLY want A but God knows best so if He says B, then FINE, I'll take B but I REALLY want A" - kind of whiny and pouty the way I hear it.

But now consider for a moment the Buddhist concept of non-attachment (that our attachments to things or outcomes are the source of suffering on this planet). Something may be enjoyable or painful, but that doesn't mean it should be pursued or avoided. If we lose something that was enjoyable, it may open the door to something even more enjoyable. And oftentimes diving deep into the pain is what is necessary to get through it, release it, and grow from it ("you cannot grow lotus flowers on marble - you have to grow them in the mud"). Just accepting things as they come along and not attaching a "this is good", "this is bad", "I want more of this", "I want less of this" judgment on them can be a pathway to inner peace and growth.

Now also consider the New Age ideas that the Universe has Infinite Intelligence that knows my good, that we are one with the creative power that is manifesting all that we desire, and that when problems come along, Ego struggles with finding a solution to the problem, while Spirit understands that the struggle IS the problem. These ideas allude to a Higher Power or a Higher Self that has a larger perspective and can be trusted to manifest exactly what we need in our lives.

Now combine these two concepts - to me this now becomes exactly what "Thy will be done" was trying to say in the first place, but without the whininess and attachment to having things look a certain way. This is the pathway to this particular Truth that works for me, and it brings me into closer alignment to the Truth than I could get with the pathway typically promulgated by the Christians. Surely the Truth, the Message, is more important than the pathway taken or the specific words used to get there.

This is just one small example among many I could give, why a multi-perspective view works better for me than a single-perspective view. Just because I see the truth and beauty in other belief systems doesn't mean I deny the truth and beauty in Christianity. And it's not just religions –

I can see how science and astrology and evolution and creation and spirituality and atheism and ecstatic dance and quantum physics and M-theory and string theory and the multiverse and dark matter and homeopathy and Masaru Emoto's water crystal experiments and shamanism and mitakuye oyasin and Indigo children and the behavior of non-Newtonian fluids and moiré patterns and chaos theory and the Mayan calendar and Schumann Resonance and theta brain waves and Atlantis and every single religion on the planet all fit together into one glorious symphony of Truth and Beauty.

None of it is contradictory to any of the rest when you take a large enough view – really quite amazing. And yet there are those who insist on listening to the beauty of only one instrument. Yes, each instrument makes beautiful sounds. And some instruments don't resonate well with some other instruments, and yet when all together in the entire symphony they somehow do.

And the symphony is glorious; now that I have heard it, a narrower perspective could never be authentic for me.

Chapter 8 - The Next Stage of Evolution

The way to see the True Path is to become conscious. More and more people are waking up as we shift into the Age of Aquarius (see chapter 12). This is part of our evolution from Homo sapiens into Homo luminous.

It has been said that what separates humans from animals is that, while animals are conscious, only humans are conscious of being conscious. It is hard to know if this statement is true. I have no way of knowing what the consciousness experience is for animals, whether they are conscious of being conscious or for that matter whether they are conscious at all. But then again, I have no way of knowing whether any human other than me is conscious.

My belief, though, is that there are at least a few species other than humans that are conscious of being conscious, and also that there are quite a few humans that are not conscious of being conscious, and many who seem to not be conscious at all. But if there is at least some truth to the statement, it implies that what allowed humans to evolve into something "more" than animals is this ability to be conscious of being conscious.

And if that is true, it would be reasonable to infer that our next stage of evolution will come about when we become conscious of being conscious of being conscious. In other words, the more we are able to stay in our witness and observe ourselves being aware of our consciousness, the faster we will evolve.

The history of the Universe is one of repeatedly evolving in stages by relinquishing autonomy to gain power and complexity. To see that this is so, let's look at the history of Everything since the beginning of Time.

According to current physics theory, about thirteen and a half billion years ago there was a Big Bang, a second or so after which the Universe consisted of densely concentrated and very hot plasma consisting of bits of energy and subatomic particles.

As the Universe expanded, it cooled until, after about 100,000 years, the plasma was cool enough to allow some of the electrons, protons and neutrons to join together stably as atoms of hydrogen and helium. By doing so, the subatomic particles lost their autonomy (they were now closely bound to other subatomic particles), but did so happily, (insofar as electrons are capable of happiness), because atoms are capable of doing so much more than subatomic particles can do.

After 200 million more years, gravity had had enough time to start collapsing regions of this hot gas into the first stars and galaxies. It was inside the nuclear furnaces of these first stars that atoms with larger nuclei were forged, as hydrogen fused into helium, and then helium fused into 100 or so other larger atoms.

Not that there weren't a few forerunners before the stars formed. In the early Universe the occasional random high speed collision might rarely result in a larger fused atomic nucleus. But the process was insignificant until stars started ramping up the process. However, during the time of the first stars atoms still existed autonomously, as the larger atoms only existed in the hearts of stars where it was too hot for chemical reactions to occur.

Most of the original hydrogen and helium didn't undergo this evolution - even today most of the atoms in the Universe are hydrogen and helium. But that small fraction of atoms that were now heavier was necessary for the next leap in evolution to take place.

When the first stars burned out their fuel supply, they exploded as supernovas. In these explosions, they spewed out the store of forged heavier atoms. These atoms would eventually form as part of new second generation stars systems, which had orbiting planetary bodies made from these larger elements.

Planets are cool enough to allow these elements to join together in stable configurations using chemical bonds, forming the first molecules.

The atoms that did this lost their autonomy, but in their place an incredibly complex array of molecules were now possible. Most of the Universe is made up of single atoms, but it's the molecules that made all the interesting bits possible. One of the most interesting bits came about with the formation of a large complex molecule called DNA that had the unique ability to replicate itself.

This set the stage for the next phase of Universal evolution: Life. For billions of years Life consisted of bacteria, single cells that were capable of much more than the random chemical reactions that had gone on before them. Different complex molecules became bound together in a cellular membrane, losing autonomy but making possible something never before seen in the Universe - organisms capable of reproducing and evolving.

For a couple of billion years on this planet life remained at the bacterial level, adapting to fill various niches from photosynthesizing cyanobacteria to thermophiles that could only live in boiling hot springs. But, overall, the bacteria were limited in how far they could evolve. Then about two billion years ago a larger amoeba-like bacterium ate a smaller bacterium but was unable to digest it.

Through a process known as symbiogenesis, the two single cells adapted to living together as one, each taking on different roles within this new hybrid cell.

The consumed bacteria produced oxygen or made vitamins, providing a survival advantage to both itself and the engulfing larger amoeba-like bacteria. Eventually the smaller bacteria became organelles called mitochondria. This loss of autonomy by the intimate joining of two single cells resulted in a new type of cell, called a eukaryotic cell, which set the stage for the next phase of Universal evolution, multicellular organisms.

About a billion years ago some single cell eukaryotic cells didn't completely split up after dividing. Eventually those cells formed conglomerations of cells all having the same DNA but specializing in specific functions by expressing only limited portions of the DNA. This loss of autonomy came with a tremendous evolutionary advantage. Although single cells far outnumber multicellular organisms, the multicellular organisms were able to reach heights far beyond what single celled organisms were capable of, and it's these multicellular organisms that do all the really interesting bits on this planet.

As multicellular organisms evolved, they reached a level of complexity that allowed groups of organisms to band together into schools, herds, and in the case of human beings, communities that grew into towns, cities, city-states, and eventually countries. Much like different cells forming specialized organs within an organism, different humans have specialized to function as specialized "organs" within the community organism. This loss of autonomy as single hunter-gatherer individuals or small family units has allowed for tremendous progress for humanity as a whole, making possible all the technological advances humans have achieved.

The pattern is obvious. Each stage of evolution is made possible by giving up autonomy and becoming a specialized part of a greater whole. But each advance is made by a smaller group that goes on to achieve far more than the greater population from which they came. There is far more hydrogen in the universe than heavier elements, but the heavier elements do all the interesting bits, just as there are far more single celled organisms than multicellular organisms, but it's the multicellular organisms that do all the interesting bits.

There is no reason to believe that this pattern won't continue, and the next major stage of evolution will be the formation of group organisms as humans give up their autonomy and become part of a greater whole. But this will likely be achieved by a small group within the greater mass of humanity, and will leave humanity in the dust in much the same way as multicellular organisms left single celled organisms behind. This will be achieved through becoming conscious of being conscious of being conscious, which is why it is so important that you are reading this book - you don't want to get left behind!

Part 2 - Waking In the Dream

Chapter 9 - What is Consciousness?

What does it mean to be conscious? We don't consider machines or computers to be conscious, no matter how complex the working parts or the program, because these things do what they do without a "driver" in a totally mechanized and predictable way. Very simple organisms such as hydras and flatworms probably can't be said to be conscious either, because their behaviors are probably as equally determined by chemistry as a computer's is by electronics or a machine's by mechanical engineering.

In addition, many actions on the parts of conscious beings such as reflexes are themselves not under conscious control. But reflexes aren't the only actions we do that are unconscious. Even complex actions such as driving a car can be unconscious; think of how many times you have hopped into your car and driven home or to work while your conscious thoughts were completely on something else or you were engrossed in a conversation with a passenger. We often drive on "autopilot" - not the car's autopilot but our own brain's.

In fact, most people's entire lives are spent on autopilot, reacting rather than acting and being totally controlled by their unconscious stories, expectations and filters. They think that they are acting consciously, but their consciousness is an illusion in the same way as someone who is asleep and dreaming is really only in a state of awareness trapped in a world created by bits of their own subconscious mind. When the dreamer wakes up, they realize that what they thought was real is now clearly a phantasm as they become conscious of the real world and their place in it.

This is very much the situation for most people in what we have thought of as the "real world". If we spend our lives reacting to events and situations unconsciously out of habit or as a result of our unconscious triggers and expectations, then our consciousness is simply along for the ride while the "dream" plays out before us. In the movie The Matrix, Morpheus asks Neo "Have you ever had a dream, Neo, that you were so sure was real? What if you were unable to wake from that dream? How would you know the difference between the dream world and the real world?"

We are each of us in a dream of our own creation from which we have (so far) not been able to awaken. The first step in becoming conscious is to realize that everything we perceive in the world around us is just a reflection of our own subconscious that we essentially create by perceiving it, and is not the actual "real world" at all, i.e. we must awaken within the "dream".

Chapter 10 - Ancient History and Its Effect on Today's Culture

Much of our subconscious programming is put in place by the culture we grow up in. Many parts of our culture came about through accidents of history and then became entrenched into our collective psyches out of habit or tradition. These things then become transparent beliefs - "truths" that are assumed without question without being able to be seen as anything other than self-evident. Culture-wide attitudes and beliefs are particularly hard to see as being merely culture-specific because they appear to be "normal", at least to most people living in that culture.

An example of this is how much and which portions of the human body are acceptable to be exposed in public. Some cultures find it immodest that any portion of a woman's body be visible in public other than a narrow slit for her eyes in her burqa. Other cultures find it self-evident that the head, arms, legs and midriff may be exposed, but certainly not the breasts or pelvic area. In Tahiti, the breasts may be exposed on the beach, but not in town. Many tribal cultures cover the pubic area but find it as bizarre to cover the breasts as a Western woman would to cover her face in public. And there are many people who are totally comfortable being completely nude in front of strangers and do not find it to be in any way sexually titillating.

All of these "norms" are culturally derived; there is no absolute level of exposure beyond which is inherently immodest. And yet people are shocked and offended when someone dresses (or undresses) below their culturally accepted norm, as though what they consider to be an acceptable level of modesty is a self-evident Truth with a capital "T".

A significant portion of our culture today derives from an event that occurred 6000 years ago and which has reverberated around the globe ever since. James DeMeo, in his book Saharasia, demonstrates clear evidence of the origins of many of today's cultural attitudes and transparent beliefs, especially those having to do with violence, child abuse, warfare, women's status in society, social hierarchies, and attitudes about sex *(SAHARASIA: THE 4000 BCE ORIGINS OF CHILD ABUSE, SEX-REPRESSION, WARFARE AND SOCIAL VIOLENCE, IN THE DESERTS OF THE OLD WORLD* by James DeMeo, Ph.D., Natural Energy Works, May 20, 2011).

DeMeo categorized cultures along a spectrum from what he calls patrist to matrist. Patrist cultures are characterized by a tendency to inflict pain and trauma upon infants and young children (such as beating children or performing mutilations such as circumcisions, clitoridectomies, and infant cranial deformation), punish young people for expressing their sexuality, force children into arranged marriages, subordinate women, and otherwise greatly restrict the freedoms of women and children to the will of males. These cultures also tend to possess high levels of adult violence and contain various social institutions that are designed for the release of pent up sadistic aggression.

At the other end of the spectrum are the peaceful matrist cultures, where child treatment and sexual relationships tend to be very gentle and pleasure oriented. Matrist cultures are also egalitarian, democratic, have a positive attitude towards sexuality, and tend to possess very low levels of adult violence.

There is little if any archeological evidence of warfare, violence, or any other behaviors characteristic of patrist culture prior to about 6000 years ago. Human culture appears to have been essentially matrist prior to that. DeMeo showed that when archeological evidence of violence and other patrist cultural behaviors are plotted on world maps over time, a clear pattern emerges, with patrist cultures appearing in North Africa, the Near East and central Asia (an area DeMeo calls Saharasia) region about 4000 to 3500 BC and then spreading out from there. Patrist cultures are found to appear later in the archeological record the further one gets from this region, until today there are almost no purely matrist societies left anywhere on the planet.

This cultural shift was precisely timed to a major historical time of climate change in this region, from relatively lush wet forests and grasslands to dry desert conditions, in exactly the time and place when human civilization was blossoming in Saharasia 6000 years ago. Cultures at the most extreme patrist end of the matrist/patrist spectrum lived in, or were strongly influenced by, people who lived in the most extreme, harsh desert environments. The actual mapped distributions of human behavior show that violent, war-making, sex-repressive and child-abusive behaviors originated within the harshest of hyperarid desert environments, and then, only about 6000 years ago.

An explanation for why these violent anti-social behaviors would appear at this time is provided by famine researchers. Famine research has shown that the emotional responses of a child to famine and starvation are similar to the emotional damage caused by maternal rejection or isolation-rearing. In other words, there are consistent psychological wounds that appear with rejection and abandonment, whether that rejection comes from one's biological mother or one's Earth-mother.

Such emotionally wounding experiences in childhood are known to have powerful disturbing effects upon later behavior in adulthood. It has been shown that people who have suffered through severe famine during childhood will then raise their own children in a different manner from prior generations, even when resources are no longer scarce. This psychological damage is not just a human problem, but one that extends to all mammals.

Infant mammals rely on something called limbic resonance to tune their limbic systems (the emotional center of the brain) to their mother's limbic system shortly after birth. Without this, mammals are incapable of forming healthy emotional responses to others. For example, infant rhesus monkeys raised in isolation without their mothers become rather cold and abusive parents themselves. They are unresponsive to the cries of their own offspring and will not pick them up and comfort them.

They also become aggressive and violent to other monkeys, including their own offspring, when caged together. These monkeys show anxious, aggressive, psychotic and depressive states that are similar to those of humans who have similar histories of abuse and rejection. And the pattern, once established, repeats itself with each generation as cycles of abuse.

When drought is severe and persistent, famine and starvations can persist for generations. At times such as this, many people die, families are destroyed, and mass migrations take place. With the focus of daily life being on survival, there are no resources left for emotionally-rich and pleasure-oriented activities and emotional bonding social activities are permanently put on the back burner. After years or generations of living this way, these behaviors become anchored into social institutions and reproduce themselves in each new generation regardless of whether or not the local resources continue to dictate such severe restrictions on behavior.

When the climate shifted and Saharasia dried up, widespread and generations-long famine resulted, and this caused culture-wide psychological core woundings when the Earth mother abandoned her children. Lack of empathy appeared as a psychological wound, and when it did, it allowed humans to engage in certain behaviors that would be abhorrent to a healthy individual, but had a survival advantage in famine-ridden Saharasia. Once the empathetic capacity was lost, however, it remained lost even after conditions no longer necessitated giving up empathy for the sake of survival, and tended to perpetuate itself.

Behaviors such as beating children, rape, circumcision, clitoridectomy, stoning people for "bad" behavior, infant cranial deformation, etc. would never have been adopted by people with a capacity for empathy. But these behaviors did in fact appear as a result of climate change and the resulting famine. The impact that the drying up of Saharasia 6000 years ago had on human culture is apparent and ongoing today.

Over time Patrist attitudes became adopted as a means of survival, and this spread from generation to generation and outward regionally in the pattern seen in DeMeo's work. A lack of resources put pressure on the culture to adopt negative attitudes towards sexual behavior as a way of controlling the population. Only children fathered by the men in control were allowed to be born, which was regulated by controlling the sexuality of the women.

Caste stratification appeared when, during mass migrations to moister regions, conquering tribes enslaved the conquered local people. Brutal practices such as infant cranial deformation started when babies were strapped to boards on their mother's backs during forced migrations to more hospitable regions, their cries of pain ignored in order to focus on survival. The resulting elongated heads then became the signature look of the conquerors, and the conquered, wanting their children to look like the ruling class, adopted the practice.

Humanity's true nature is thus not of violence and warfare; these things came about as a result of climate change. To see our true nature, we need only look to what unarmored matrist cultures are (or were) like. Matrist cultures are characterized by more physical affection with children, no painful initiations with children, a permissive pleasurable attitude toward sexuality, absence of genital mutilations (circumcision, clitoridectomy), no female virginity taboo, no intercourse taboos, freely permitted adolescent lovemaking, equal status for women, females having the freedom to choose their own mate or divorce at will, democratic and egalitarian social structures, nonviolence, and an absence of strict codes of behavior.

When we take into account the historical impact of the climate change in Saharasia, we can see that many of our cultural norms are really just a result of a core wounding on a humanity-wide level (for one example of how a cultural norm of today has been influenced by the drying of Saharasia, see chapter 11). Matrist attitudes are in fact representative of humanity's natural unwounded state. By recognizing where unhealthy patrist attitudes originate, we are freed to choose healthier alternatives, and no longer be at the mercy of subconscious programming.

Chapter 11 - Relationships

One of our culturally programmed transparent beliefs concerns what relationships should look like. When patrist attitudes became the norm, emphasis was put on monogamy as the model for how relationships should be (see chapter 10). This was because in the face of dwindling resources, a man would be willing to expend those resources raising a child only if he knew it was his, and so restrictions were put in place on who the women could have sex with.

Relationships became defined by fidelity, to the point where a break in fidelity generally has meant the end of the relationship. But if humans were naturally supposed to be monogamous, breaks in fidelity wouldn't be nearly as common as we find them to be. I've done the monogamy thing, and have been burned repeatedly by my partners cheating on me. And I discovered that I was far from being alone in this situation.

A recent UK survey (the Way We Are Now nationwide survey conducted by the marriage guidance counseling organization Relate) revealed that 34% of women are having or have had an affair after having children - these are mothers who are supposed to be setting an example for and protecting their children, yet engaging in behavior that once discovered very often ends up leading to divorce.

I finally realized that it's society that wants monogamy - not necessarily the individuals within society. But because society demands that we can only be attracted to one person at a time, when people do feel an attraction to someone other than their partner, they are left with either stuffing it, which will tend to resurface later in unhealthy ways, or to act on it in a hurtful dishonest manner.

I've spent a good portion of my life trying to find a better path, and what has worked for me was to question the assumption that True Love must be monogamous, to deal with attractions in an open honest way and not cheat or stuff it. Consequently, I've been exploring what it is like to have a more polyamorous relationship, which has lead me to finding and helping build a polyamorous community.

I am surrounded by lots of unrestricted love and when it works it feels great and natural. It certainly doesn't always go smoothly, and jealousy is frequently a challenge. But my wife and I do sometimes date others and have very close loving relationships with our friends (and are very honest with each other about all these relationships), and yet we are totally committed to each other and always put our relationship first.

In fact, our commitment feels stronger since we don't base our commitment on fidelity, but simply on the fact that we choose to be together. I've seen infidelity destroy too many otherwise good relationships, and it's a shame because it doesn't have to be that way. But society has ingrained into us that if we cheat or are attracted to another, our relationship must be over.

For those who question my conclusion that monogamy is not what is natural for humans, consider this: if we are naturally monogamous, we're just about the only species that is so. Genetic testing has revealed that monogamy in nature is a myth. Ninety-nine percent of mammal species never form lasting pair-bonds (Discover Magazine, April, 2008). Those that do form lasting bonds continue to bear illegitimate offspring - as many as 80 percent of them, in the case of the "monogamous" red fox.

Adelie penguins are famously monogamous, yet females occasionally slip away from their mates to couple with unattached males. They apparently charge for this service - stones to add to the nest. Whether this is best viewed as prostitution or child support isn't clear, but the case against monogamy is.

When a male goose courts another male goose, a female will sometimes slip in and mate with both of the males. The male partners will then later share paternal duties. So here in nature is an example of a triad - it's not just humans doing these "weird" things. Monogamy is not "natural", it is an unnatural behavior imposed upon us by society, with dangerous results. It is only by being true to our authentic selves that we can reach our highest potential. We must love as we were meant to, or continue to suffer with cheating and dishonesty.

In conventional society, saying "I'm married" implies a whole set of rules about behaviors that are now off-limits. Among the people I socialize with, however, it would simply be a statement of fact such as "my eyes are blue" and would in no way imply that the speaker cannot be flirted with or dated or propositioned. If any of those things were done in conventional society, the speaker would be offended or even shocked, for they clearly said that they were married. In my social group though, it would just be expected that if they didn't want to date or copulate with them, they would simply politely turn them down, with no judgment on the propositioner.

Non-monogamous relationships do take a lot of work, but most of that work involves undoing social programming. The work required is often too much for some people, so non-monogamy is not for everyone. But for those willing to put the effort into relearning how to relate, non-monogamy, done ethically, can save relationships rather than destroy them.

Chapter 12 - Wounding Through the Ages

The Earth wobbles on its axis very slowly, taking 25,920 years to complete one circuit. This corresponds to the "Great Year" of the Mayan calendar, which came to an end on December 21, 2012 when the earth, sun and center of the galaxy lined up for the first time in nearly 26,000 years. As the wobble progresses, the constellations against which the sun sits on the Spring Equinox changes, shifting backward through the zodiac, changing signs every 2100 to 2200 years.

Each of these is called an "Age", and each Age is associated with characteristics associated with that sign. Transitions from one age to the next often occur with some disruptions, with particularly large disruptions occurring with shifts into one of the four Fixed Signs (Scorpio, Leo, Taurus, and Aquarius).

Lack of empathy and compassion for others can initiate core woundings in the recipient. Different degrees of lack of empathy will lead to different core wounds. Individuals with limited empathetic capacities can only comprehend the behavior of others who are at or below their level.

I believe this is true for humanity just as it is for the individual human. There was a disaster thousands of years ago that lead to a deep core wound in humanity as a whole, which resulted in a loss of empathic capacity in humans (see chapter 10). Each Age has seen a lessening of the degree of general lack of empathy as the lessons of the New Age attempt to heal the wounding from the Prior Age.

In addition, there are humanity-wide core wounds that are associated with each Age, which themselves are caused by and perpetuate different degrees of lack of empathy and compassion for others. Just as deep core wounds can be inflicted on a child whose parents lack the empathetic capacity to treat them with compassion, I believe there are archetypal woundings for humanity as a whole that are associated with the level of empathetic capacity that corresponds with each particular Age.

13,000 years ago the last ice age came to an end, and with it the end of the Age of Virgo. The sign of Virgo is associated with discernment, and perhaps this was a time when humans started to perceive the universe in a deeper way. With the ending of the Age of Virgo around 11,000 BCE came the Age of Leo, one of the Fixed Signs, and it ushered in a major change in the human condition.

Leo is associated with creativity, playfulness, performance, confidence, and being showy. As the ice curtain lifted, the Earth became warmer and life was less of a struggle for survival. Leo came out to play, and to perform on the new stage that appeared as the ice receded. Humans had had to cooperate to survive the ice, and that cooperation fostered a strong sense of empathy that remained with mankind into the Age of Leo, and there was no core wounding present at this time.

Then about 8600 BCE the sun entered Cancer, and humanity's Age of Cancer began. Cancer is associated with the Archetypal Mother, the Drinker of Life. The Earth continued to warm, and the sea levels rose. This was a time of great bounty, when the Earth provided well for Her people. At this time the Sahara, the Middle East and southwest Asia were moist and lush, a veritable Garden of Eden that supported humanity's development of agriculture and living in larger communities. It was the height of the Earth-based goddess religions, as people came to recognize that the Earth provided its bounty to Her people as a mother provides for her children.

There may have been a dark side to the Age of Cancer, in that as much as the Earth was providing, the Sea was taking away. The hunter-gatherers would tend to build their settlements near coastlines, as is true today (about two-thirds of humanity now lives within 400km of a coastline). Sea levels rose 300 feet when the great ice sheets retreated, drowning the settlements within a few generations of their being established. Though the Earth was bountiful, the Sea destroyed our homes, but this was probably not enough to cause a core wounding for humanity, as needing to move the community inland a few hundred feet is not as devastating as a regional famine.

The next Age was the Age of Gemini, which lasted from about 6450 BCE to about 4300 BCE. Gemini is associated with transformative thought, communication, networks, and translating. This was the time when humans learned to domesticate livestock, surely a transformative notion in our developing culture. Trade with other regions grew, establishing networks with other peoples, who often spoke different languages that needed to be translated to be understood.

There may have been a dark side to the Age of Gemini, such as humans abandoning the hunter-gatherer way of life, trading a simpler and freer way of life for the steady but labor-intensive food supply of agriculture. But at this point in our development there is no archeological evidence of warfare, violence, or child abuse (such as cranial deformation), and I believe that humans were still basically peaceful, cooperative and emotionally healthy.

The end of the Age of Gemini ushered in one of the fixed signs, the Age of Taurus, lasting from about 4300 BCE to about 2150 BCE, and the Age of Taurus brought with it another major shift in the condition of humanity. It was during the Age of

Taurus that the lush forests and grasslands of the Sahara, Middle East and southwest Asia began to dry up. Suddenly the supportive Mother Earth was no longer supporting Her children, there was widespread famine and starvation, and this had a profound impact on our subsequent history, as discussed in chapter 10.

Thus did the Age of Taurus bring with it a core wounding of humanity that resulted from abandonment by our Earth-mother. When children are raped, mutilated, and used as objects or possessions without regard for their emotional wellbeing, the damage done is felt for the rest of their lives and passed on to future generations. It is a hopeless state, for the child is powerless to change their situation, which is reflected by humanity's powerlessness to change their once lush Eden from becoming a desiccated wasteland.

The sign of Taurus is characterized by stubbornness, abundance, and wealth, and though this does not sound much like the conditions 6000 years ago, it is interesting to note that this was the time period when archeologists began to find evidence of grave-wealth and castes and divine-kingships. As resources became scarce, those in power began to gather wealth from those "below" them, and hoard the wealth against future lean times.

This is similar to hoarding behavior often seen in people who lived through the Great Depression, despite living in abundance in later years. Therefore, the "wealth" of the Taurian Age is the wealth of the few at the expense of the many, hoarded out of fear of lack of abundance.

This was the Age when lack of empathetic capacity entered the world, and the resulting humanity-wide issues of warfare, violence, subjugation of women, abuse of children, taboos on who and how we love, and sex-negativity. This is the source of the humanity-wide wound we are still healing from (see chapter 10).

The earth's axis continued its wobble until the Spring Equinox sun entered the constellation of Aries, ushering in the Arian Age which lasted from about 2150 BCE until about 1 CE. Aries is characterized as a warrior, a go-getter, courageous, daring, angry and fiery. The Age of Aries is also the start of the Bronze Age, when fire was used to smelt metal into weapons of war, which gave the desert people a tremendous advantage in conquering surrounding lands.

The Arian Age tried to heal the wounding that came about in the Taurian Age. As human's capacity for empathy started to re-expand, those individuals who were on the forefront of this expansion could perceive the harm that was being done by uncompassionate behaviors and did what they could to stop it by codifying rules of behavior. This level of empathy is characterized by the parent or authority figure giving rules to the child or to those "beneath" them, which must be followed in order to avoid punishment.

This is a step up from the prior level of abandonment and abuse, in that there is now some means of control of one's fate, for one can now hope to avoid abuse by obeying the rules. The Age of Aries was the time of Moses, the law-giver, and he exemplified the mind-set of this Age. He ushered in the (then) New Age of Ares (the ram, then represented by sacrificing lambs to God), and was angry when the Israelites worshiped the golden calf (i.e. holding on to the old paradigm of the Age of Taurus, the bull).

This is the paradigm still held by those who hold to fundamentalist religions, who insist on everybody obeying the Law of God (as they interpret it) or risk burning in Hell for eternity. Repressive as this way of thinking is, it was an improvement over the human condition in the Age of Taurus, as forcing people to obey a set of reasonable rules provided some stability in a culture devoid of empathy and compassion for others.

If somebody is so unfeeling that they don't see that abuse, murder, torture, rape, etc. are not acceptable things to do, then there is something deeply wrong with that person and they need a fundamentalist type of religion; unfortunately, fundamentalists tend not to realize that not everybody is that deeply wounded.

For the past 2000 or so years the sun has been in Pisces. Pisces is characterized by sensitiveness, spirituality, transforming to what's next, dissolving, and channeling. The Age of Pisces was also the Age of Christianity, which is why there are so many fish symbols in Christianity (the fish symbol so frequently seen on bumpers, feeding the masses with two fish, Jesus choosing fishermen for disciples).

Jesus exemplified the mind-set of Pisces just as Moses had for Aries. With Christianity we start seeing a picture of a more loving less vengeful God. With the appearance of Patrist culture in the Age of Taurus, God shifted from female to male and from below (the mother-Earth goddess) to above. Pisces is still about God-from-above, but this, along with many other ways of thinking and being, will be dissolving and transforming with the Age of Aquarius.

The empathetic capacity associated with the Age of Pisces is Reward for Performance. The message is that you can be loved if you are good, rather than just not-punished. This is the message our schools give out – study hard and you'll get good grades.

This is also the message of Christmas – be good and Santa will bring you lots of presents.

In fact, much of the mindset of our culture in the Age of Pisces is steeped in this level of empathy. The cultural wound is the same as the wound children receive when raised with this mindset, the idea that love is conditional. Again, though, this is an improvement over the last level, for here for the first time there is enough empathy to allow love to be considered part of the equation.

The sun is now moving into the sign of Aquarius, another Fixed Sign, with another major shift in consciousness expected. Aquarius is the rebel, the reformer, the revolutionary. It is about cosmic consciousness and ideas that lead to change. These things should give an idea of what we have in store ahead of us. The years just ahead of us will be about new ways of thinking that will lead to revolutionary changes in how people interact as we shift our consciousness to the cosmic plane.

I also expect that with the Age of Aquarius we will find our empathetic capacity expanding once more. This will, again, be an improvement over the prior Age as we try to heal the wounds generated during the Age of Pisces. There will also be a corresponding shadow side to challenge us.

This expanded sphere of empathetic capacity is characterized by encouraging and guiding each individual in finding and expressing their uniqueness. This is again an improvement over the last Age of conditional love, but there will be a dark side to this as well. The shadow side of the Aquarian empathetic capacity is that the individual is not trusted to be able to find their own way and is seen as needing guidance.

It is hard to say exactly how this will manifest for humanity as a whole, but one possible scenario could be that aliens will intervene in the affairs of mankind just in the nick of time before we destroy ourselves or our environment. Though it would be nice to be rescued from the deepening mess we are finding ourselves in, I could see that such an action would have the effect that we would come to believe that we weren't good enough or clever enough to do it without them.

The dominant religions of each Age have, at their core, the level of empathy that corresponds to that Age, as they try to heal the wounding from the last Age. This is represented by the shadow side of the next lower level, while the challenge for the individual living in that Age is to bring the next higher level into themselves. Thus, in the Age of Aries we had the Ten Commandments, which tried to heal the abandonment and abuse that appeared in the Age of Taurus with the drying up of Saharasia, while the challenge for the individuals was to feel good about themselves for obeying the Law (rather than to just feel relieved that they were not being punished).

In the Age of Pisces we had Christianity, which tried to heal the excessive control of the Age of Aries by showing that loving your neighbor as yourself was what was important, and the Laws would follow naturally from that, while the challenge for the individual has been to find their unique path in that process.

In the Age of Aquarius we will shift from God (male)-from-above to Spirit (genderless)-from-within as we grow into our unique place in the cosmos and try to heal the wounding from the Age of Pisces with unconditional love. The challenge for individuals in the Age of Aquarius will be to become unified with all of their different parts.

In Moses' time it was about the Law - what we physically did with our bodies. This was where our sense of self was and the part that had to change to get into Heaven or ascend to higher planes.

Jesus brought what had to change to a deeper level - how we felt, thought and reacted within our skulls. He said "Love thy neighbor as thyself" and that if you "do unto others as your would have them do unto you", following the Law would naturally follow. Regain the empathy that was lost in order to ascend to higher planes. We had to change ourselves now on the level of our sense of self at that time - our psyches.

The next level of self beyond our psyches is our Organic Self, which is basically who we would have been if we had never been wounded. This is where the next level of change must occur, in order to bring our sense of self to the layer that underlies that - the Oneness of All.

Chapter 13 - Who Are You, Really?

To what exactly are you referring when you say or think "I". Is it your clothes and outward persona you present to others? Is it your physical body? Or is it your memories? Or your thoughts, triggers and emotions? Or does the concept of "I" for you encompass not only all of this but also extend beyond to include the reality you create around you through your perceptions and expectations?

All of these things are reasonable definitions of "you", to varying depths and degrees. But at the same time none of these things are really "you".

You are certainly not the clothes or outward persona you put on, for you can change your clothes or act differently and still feel like the same you. Neither are you your physical body. There isn't a single atom in your body that was there 7 years ago, not in your brain, not in your DNA; like a wave traveling across the ocean which briefly incorporates individual water molecules into its "body" as it passes by, our bodies are simply a wave form, albeit a much more complex one, that temporarily incorporates individual atoms and molecules for varying but ultimately temporary periods of time as we roll through our existence.

If you lose an appendix through surgery, or cut off your hair or trim your fingernails, you don't feel any less of a "you". So you are not your physical body – that is simply something you are wearing in much the same way as you put on a persona or wear an outfit.

What about memories? If we lose our memory for a period of time in our lives, it can indeed feel as though that portion of our selves that experienced that time in our life has "died". With complete amnesia, you may feel like "you", but a "you" disconnected from the you that existed in the past. Nevertheless, we are much more than the sum total of our memories.

If you get really drunk one night and the next morning have no recollection of the antics you performed in your debauchery, you don't believe that you weren't you during that period, especially after viewing the photographic evidence pasted all over the internet the next day. And memories are very often found to be inaccurate and sometimes downright fabricated. Does this make "you" inaccurate or fabricated? Perhaps, but this tends to not be our experience.

So let's dive deeper in search of the real "you". Thoughts and feelings, emotional baggage, all of those parts of the psyche that give us the flavor of our conscious experience tend to feel like who we are at a very deep level. Nevertheless, I maintain that even this level is not yet the core essence of "you".

We can change our minds and not feel as though we are suddenly a different person. We can feel an emotion so strongly that it seems in that moment that that is all that we are, but we also have the ability to step back consciously from that emotion, observe ourselves having a feeling, evaluate its appropriateness, recognize what core wound is being triggered, and chose to alter our response all without ever feeling as though we are now somebody else.

Our psyche can change with therapy, with drugs, with brain damage, with spiritual experiences, but throughout it all you still feel like you. An emotional response to something is still something that on some level you are choosing to wear like an article of clothing, and with enough self-awareness can be changed just as easily.

Finally, there is the theory that everything, ultimately, is you. People will often experience this during deep meditation or while under the influence of certain psychedelic pharmaceuticals, especially if one can go so deep as to experience "ego death" wherein temporarily there is no more concept of an "I" and all that is left to identify with is absolutely everything else in the entire universe, and one feels a oneness with all that is (see chapter 24).

Quantum theory also alludes to this, stating that every possible state of being exists simultaneously as a probability wave, and only collapses into one state of being at the moment it is observed. Thus, all of observed reality is a direct consequence of an observer observing, which makes the observer an utterly integral part of the entire universe (or at least of the observer's personal universe).

Nevertheless, your personal reality is not you. It is the moiré pattern created by the interaction of the wave pattern that is "you" (or your perspective) and the wave pattern of all that is not you (see chapter 16).

So who, then, are you? Who am I? I am reminded of an experience I once had shortly after I first moved to Portland. In the center of downtown Portland stands the US Bank Building, a large pink skyscraper commonly referred to as "Big Pink". Near the top is a fancy restaurant with amazing views of the entire city in every direction. Some friends brought us to have drinks there, but at the time, being new to Portland, I didn't realize that the US Bank building was "Big Pink".

As I went from window to window enjoying the view and picking out the landmarks I recognized, I kept looking for Big Pink, but couldn't seem to find it anywhere, naturally, because I was in it. This is similar in a way to the search for ourselves – we look out at our bodies, our feelings, our memories, all the different "buildings" that make up the city of "I". But, the core central building keeps eluding us because we don't realize we are so deeply in it that we have difficulty recognizing it.

We need a change in perspective in order to see that who we are, at our very core, is simply our perspective: the unattached observer that watches us cry, watches us hurt, watches us remember, but isn't itself affected by any of those things. The immortal words of Buckaroo Bonsai said it best: "No matter where you go, there you are". That "you" that is always there - no matter where you go or where you look - is the real you.

Chapter 14 - The Rainbow Perspective

The universe is infinitely large. At the same time, the core essence of who we are, our perspective (see chapter 13), is an infinitely small point. How ironic that that one infinitesimal point is, at least in our personal universe, the most important point in that universe. The entire rest of the universe becomes defined by that one tiny point (at least, again, in our own personal universe).

Rainbows offer us a simple example of the importance of that single infinitesimal point of perspective, and how we create our own personal reality around us centered on that point. When there is a rainbow in the sky, it appears to be something "out there" that we can point out to someone standing next to us. They can see what we assume is the same rainbow, and we can all agree that the rainbow is indeed there "in the sky".

The fact is, however, that we all see our own personal rainbow. That rainbow only exists within our heads, and no two people can ever see exactly the same rainbow.

Rainbows are created when different wavelengths of light get refracted to different degrees as they pass through raindrops, which act as little prisms. The actual rainbow that we see results from the interaction of the sunlight, the raindrops, and our eyeballs. The colors that fall on our retina appear there thanks to the precise angle formed by the sun, the raindrops and our eyes. Thus, rainbows always form a perfect circle (or portion of a circle) the center of which is exactly opposite the sun from our head.

In other words, the center of the rainbow circle is always where the shadow of our head would be cast by the sun. Should we take a step to the right or left, the shadow of our head moves slightly, and the position of the rainbow in the sky also shifts accordingly. We actually see a slightly different rainbow when we move to the side, each centered on a slightly different point.

Both rainbows, along with an infinite number of other rainbows, exist at the same time, not as separate definable rainbows but rather as a mish mash of overlapping potential rainbows, more like a ball of wibbly wobbly timey wimey rainbow stuff (see chapter 32). The one that we end up seeing depends on where we happen to be standing. All of the other rainbows are also there, just waiting to coalesce into "existence".

This "coalescing out of the mish mash of wibbly wobbly timey wimey potentialities" is exactly what happens when Reality is created by our observation (see chapter 30). We are always at the center of our personal rainbows in the same way that a singularity is always at the center of the black hole or the observer is always at the center of the universe, and all for the same reason.

Chapter 15 - Who Will Do the Driving?

One should act from that part that is best qualified to do the acting. We are made up of all our past experiences - all stacked on top of each other. If we pass through like a flip book, we get the illusion that we are moving through time.

Sometimes we encounter situations that resonate deeply with one particular slice of this stack of experiences, say one from when we were six years old. That particular slice may feel reminded of some past emotional wound by the situation. We get triggered. And react as if we were six years old again, with the skill set of a six-year-old, as that part of us tries to protect us from being wounded again in that same way.

But a six-year-old's skill set is not as well equipped to handle the situation as most of our more adult slices are. We handle the situation better if we act from our more adult self rather than letting our inner six-year-old take over. That doesn't mean to walk all over our inner six-year-old, but rather to honor it and give it compassion. Help it feel safe, but don't let it drive.

According to Carl Jung, the parts of our psyche that we don't deal with within us, we manifest in the world outside us to deal with there (see chapter 21).

When something becomes an issue for us in our outside world, it is worth looking at to see if it is a reflection of an issue we are not looking at in our inside world.

For example, a very important issue for me is honoring different perspectives and giving voice to different people's viewpoints. I tend to get triggered when someone acts as though their perspective is the True perspective and tries to push that perspective onto others. Since this is an issue for me, it may be that I actually may not be honoring all of the different parts of my inner psyche, and I will continue to see this problem in my outside world as long as I continue to not give voice to all the different parts of me.

People generally agree that it isn't right for one individual or group to force their will onto another individual or group. We should all have the freedom to have our own voices and live authentically, as long as doing so doesn't interfere with the voices and freedoms of others. Obviously we cannot allow someone to go on a killing rampage, no matter how "authentic" that might be for them, so we must strike a balance between the needs of the individual and the needs of society. But in general it is good to honor the needs of the individual and allow society to benefit from the collective voices of all of its members.

This is also true of all the voices within us. It is no more right to force the will of one part of us over another than it is for one person to force their will onto another. There may be some wounded inner child within us whose issues the other parts of us just cannot bear. But it does no good to "suck it up" and ignore that part.

Just as we want to treat all members of society with compassion, we should treat all of our wounded inner parts with compassion as well. And just as society doesn't let a wounded individual go on a killing rampage, we also shouldn't let those wounded inner parts take over to the detriment of the rest of ourselves. Compassion is one thing, but again the proper balance must be reached. Integration of all our inner parts, with compassion for each, is how our inner society functions best.

We are more than just the sum of all of our past experiences. We are also made up of our future experiences, our experiences in our past lives, the experiences of our higher selves, the experiences of our potential selves, etc. Sometimes we encounter a situation that would be best handled by one of these other selves. At those times, it is best to get out of our own way and let a more qualified self take the wheel, rather than try to handle it with the limited skill set that we currently have mastered.

Chapter 16 - Moiré Patterns and Reality

Moiré patterns are interference patterns produced when two (or more) fields of repetitive patterns overlap and produce a new pattern which was not present in either of the original patterns. Very simple patterns are produced when two sets of identical parallel lines are superimposed with one set inclined at a slight angle to the other. More complex patterns appear with more complex, non-linear base patterns.

These patterns also show up when looking at two window screens placed on top of each other, looking at one cyclone fence through another cyclone fence, etc. (see the chair-back example below). Moiré patterns mostly show up in our daily lives as an undesired artifact of images produced by various digital imaging and computer graphics techniques.

Example of Moiré patterns produced by two overlapping mesh fabrics on the backs of chairs.

Obviously, the more complex and non-linear the base patterns (in both space and time), the more complex can be the resulting moiré pattern.

So what does all this have to do with the nature of reality? The universe was created when the concept "I am" (or "Self") appeared out of the quantum flux (along with its anti-concept "I am not" or "Not Self"). (Just as particles and anti-particles, such as electrons and positrons, can appear at random out of the quantum flux and quickly annihilate each other, I believe that concepts and anti-concepts can also appear at random out of the quantum flux).

Everything - all matter, all energy, even concepts - is wave patterns. In the case of concepts, the wave pattern is most easily seen as a brainwave pattern visualized on an EEG when the brain conceptualizes something, but this brainwave pattern is probably a reflection of a wave pattern inherent in the concept itself. When the wave pattern of "Self" is superimposed on the wave pattern of "Not Self", it creates an artificial moiré pattern. It is this pattern that is the actual "physical universe" that we observe around us. The physical universe doesn't actually exist in and of itself. It is simply a by-product of the interaction of our perspective and that which we view as outside ourselves.

The true nature of the Universe is not the "reality" we perceive. It is, instead, an infinitely complex overlapping waveform of possibilities (see chapter 30). Sense is made of this mish-mash by our conscious observation of the mish-mash, which causes a particular wave-form to coalesce out as a moiré pattern resulting from the interaction of the wave-forms of the multiverse and the wave-form of our consciousness.

What we observe the universe to be is actually an artifact of the interaction of these two wave-forms, one of which can be altered by changing our perspective. So what is the "true" nature of reality? A natural assumption is that it is the mish-mash of possibilities existing as a complex wave-form that represents the infinite possible ways the Universe can be.

But this ignores the other half of the reality equation; our consciousness is in fact the "true" nature of the universe. The mish-mash is the background upon which it resides. And "reality" is just our consciousness's way of trying to make sense of the background mish-mash.

What this all implies is that we can change the nature of our perceived reality around us simply by changing our perspective; altering our point of view will have a direct effect on the base pattern of our Self-field, which will shift the moiré patterns and have a direct effect on the physical universe around us.

So how does one shift one's perspective, especially to the point of altering reality? There are many ways, including meditation (see chapter 24), ecstatic dance (see chapter 23), near-death experiences, psychedelics (especially hallucinogenic mushrooms, DMT and LSD) (see chapter 27), identifying and changing one's transparent beliefs, and psychotherapy.

Some of these methods may have a temporary but intense effect (e.g. psychedelics). Others may require years of commitment (e.g. meditation). The best path depends on the individual as well as the type of reality-change one is hoping to achieve. For example, a level-1 reality change, such as manifesting a parking space, would likely necessitate using very different methods than a level-3 reality change, such as levitating (see chapter 30).

One of the problems with perspective change is that our perspective tends to be fairly well rooted in place. We may be able to lean way over for a new perspective temporarily, but afterwards we tend to shift back to our old known and comfortable perspective. One good way to achieve more permanent perspective-change is through ego-death.

Ego-death (losing the sense of "I", leaving one with only the sense of "not-I" and a feeling of oneness with the entire universe) is most frequently achieved in deep meditative states or through the use of high doses of hallucinogenic mushrooms. However it is achieved, if there is no intention set prior to the experience, the tendency will be to either return to the prior perspective state or to achieve a new but random perspective state. But with proper intention-setting preparation, ego-death can be an effective method of "re-booting" one's psyche with the result of shifting reality in a specific planned fashion.

Chapter 17 - The Pattern and the Interpretation

Reality is very much a subjective entity, as is repeatedly shown by quantum physics. That's not to say that it is entirely subjective, but rather that subjectivity plays an integral role in the creation of reality. The conceptualization of the world around us is our own personal reality that is created inside our heads.

We like to believe that it corresponds in some meaningful and accurate way to some external reality "out there". And likely it does. But there is no way for any one of us to personally determine this, because once we observe or understand anything about the theoretical outside world, it becomes part of our conceptualization and is no longer "out there".

We might ask others what Reality looks like to them and compare their story to our own for confirmation. But even these external confirmations come to us via our sense organs, and are themselves subject to the same filters, expectations and reinterpretations that we use when we observe the world around us. We can't know anything about a completely external reality without taking ourselves out of the equation, and once we do that we no longer can personally know anything about the world around us.

Of course, you may say that you can observe me observing the world around me, and compare that to what you observe when I'm gone, and thus confirm to me that the external reality that I think I observe is pretty much what's there without me. But the problem is that both your observation of my view of the world and your observation of the world around me are taking place in your head. Both are part of your personal reality and may have little to do with the reality going on inside of my head.

So it becomes meaningless to talk of an external reality separate from ourselves. All we can really talk about is our personal realities, which overlap in many ways with each others', but are all unique and differ from each others' - often in significant ways.

As I see it, there are two components to reality: the pattern of signals entering our consciousness, and our conscious interpretation of those signals. Each of these components, the Pattern and the Interpretation, can be described as a waveform, and these waveforms interact to form a moiré pattern which is our personal reality (see chapter 16).

Pattern recognition is part of the automatic circuitry that occurs below the level of consciousness, in our subconscious (it essentially defines the subconscious). Everything we recognize in the world around us exists within our heads as a neural network of pattern recognition, or we wouldn't be able to "see" it.

Thus, it is our subconscious that allows us to create our perceived reality. Without it, all would be just patterns of incoming signals.

There is something on the order of 20 million afferent nerve fibers bringing information about the outside world into our brains. The firing (or not firing) of each of those fibers creates a pattern that our brains use to interpret what is going on around us.

A 1080i HD video screen has a frame size (in pixels) of 1920 X 1080 (W X H), giving just over 2,000,000 pixels per image. 10 HD video screens could display all of the information from all of our senses coming into our brain. Some of those pixels would represent visual signals from our eyes, while other pixels might represent information about sounds from our auditory nerve fibers, odors, the position of our body in space, or that ache in our lower back.

Our entire moment to moment experience could theoretically be represented as an ever-changing pattern on those ten video screens. The brain is very good at seeing patterns and meaning in data. It is this ability that makes it possible to distinguish a brain from a computer.

A brain has the ability to interpret those verification codes that some internet websites require you to read and type back that verifies that you are a human. The brain can somehow immediately make sense of those smeared and distorted numbers and letters whereas we have yet to be able to program a computer to make sense of those things.

The brain will take in a surprisingly small amount of data points, and then fill in the gaps to create a complete picture in our heads (see chapter 37). We sample a tiny fraction of the available data about the world around us and we proceed to construct in our minds a working approximation that is generally accurate enough to serve us pretty well, though it can often be fooled, for example when it is purposefully done to create illusions.

When we dream, it is this story-making ability of the brain that is running wild, unplugged from the stream of inputs coming from our afferent nerve fibers and creating stories instead from random inputs that bubble up from our subconscious. This free-running interpretation/story-making ability creates dream realities in our heads that seem just as real to us while we're in the dream as waking reality is to us when we are awake.

You are probably familiar with the optical illusion that can look like either a vase or two faces (see the figure below). This is an example of seeing the pattern (really, just a glob of black ink on a white background) or the interpretation (which in this case shifts from "vase" to "faces"). This illusion shows us the degree to which our brains are wired to put an interpretation on things.

It's very easy to shift back and forth from one story to another, from seeing a vase to seeing two faces. It's very hard to see both simultaneously - our brains fall into one state (a state of seeing faces) to another (a state of seeing a vase) but not both at the same time, much like falling into one well or another but not both at the same time (see chapter 24).

It's hard to see one perspective when you're seeing another. It's also hard to not see either a vase or faces; a pattern without a story is meaningless and our brains crave meaning and so put stories on everything.

We can practice seeing both the vase and the two faces simultaneously. Try staring at the picture until you can see both. It may help to picture it as two heads holding a vase between them.

Doing this can help train the brain into being able to see multiple interpretations simultaneously, a useful skill that can help us keep from getting caught up in one story.

We can also practice seeing the pattern, that is, neither faces nor a vase. This is even harder to do, but once accomplished, can help train our brain into being able to just discern what is without judgment - without attaching a story or even a name. There are many layers of stories that can be untold.

At its deepest, without any stories whatsoever, we would just BE with the simple awareness of the neural input entering our brains. This would be a place of incredible power, for we would be able to choose how we perceive our world. Without being stuck down one well of perception (for example, a vase well or a faces well), we would have all the possibilities laid out before us for us to pick from. We would be free to pick the most beautiful interpretation.

Chapter 18 - Moiré Patterns and Time

"Reality" is a moiré pattern resulting from the superimposition of the "self" wave pattern with the "not self" wave pattern (see chapter 16).

Motion results from the shifting of the two wave patterns relative to each other. I once came across a children's book with some very cleverly made clear gels with carefully placed wavy lines on them. The two gels superimposed on top of each other caused the lines to create a moiré pattern that would look like, say, a horse, and when the gels were moved relative to each other the horse would appear to run.

Since time is meaningless without motion, time itself does not exist but is an illusion resulting from the interaction of the "self" and "not self" wave patterns.

If two patterns are identical in every respect to each other, including orientation, there can be no moiré pattern generated from their superimposition. This is why, in deep meditative states or psychedelic experiences when one feels "at one" with the universe, the "self" and "not self" wave patterns become identical. The moiré pattern called "reality" and the illusion called "time" cease to exist. We become aware of the quantum flux, but the experience seems to be timeless (i.e. lasting infinitely long in an instant).

Chapter 19 - The Nature of Evil

People often wonder about why there is so much evil in the world, and often attribute the presence of Evil to the work of evil supernatural beings – Satan, Mara, etc. I have some thoughts as to where Evil is really coming from.

As people start to come into their power, start to wake up from the Dream and become conscious, they go through a transition phase wherein they start to see all the connections. Everything starts to have meaning. Messages start to come through from their higher selves.

This sometimes happens transiently with psychedelics (see chapter 27) or other perspective-shifting practices such as Dance (see chapter 23). But when the drugs wear off or the dance is over, we are often left with half-memories, and attribute the impressions we received as an effect of the drug or the dance.

Once back in our "normal" state, we perceive that the meanings and messages are reflections of our higher selves: microcosms of greater macrocosms - the Metaconscious speaking through someone who may have no conscious awareness as to the nature of the message they are relaying.

Eventually we reach a stage where we realize that all of reality, the Good and the Evil, is created by the act of our perceiving it. Everyone we meet, every event that we perceive, is manifested into being as a reflection of some part of our subconscious (see chapter 15).

When we wonder why there is Evil in the world, we realize it is there because we created it, not because of the acts of a supernatural being. We are Satan, even as we are God.

This is why it is so important for people who become activated, who want to learn about coming into their power, to do the work on themselves. If we learn to shift reality and become powerful beings, we must be careful to not give that power to the parts of our subconscious that creates Evil in the world - at least until we have healed that part - or Satan will become ever more powerful in the world.

Chapter 20 - Heaven and Hell

If the purpose of Hell is to scare us into good behavior, then surely it is the threat of Hell rather than Hell itself that is the important thing - much like the threat that the boogie man will "get" the child if the child doesn't behave doesn't require an actual boogie man in order to be effective.

And much like it would take a cruel and sadistic parent to allow an actual boogie man (whatever that is) to hurt their child should their behavior not improve, so would it be inconsistent with a loving God to make good on the threat of Hell for those who don't strike up some sort of a deal with Him during their lifetime. (Or for that matter those who do strike up a deal but get the name wrong).

No, the concept of Hell as a punishment for non-believers of a just, loving and all-powerful God makes no sense.

We are living under the delusion that we are all separate individuals. If during our time on this planet we act selfishly, hurt each other, steal from each other, judge others as being "bad", etc., then when we die, re-integrating back into the Whole and suddenly feeling all the hurts and negative judgments we have done and had towards what turns out to be other aspects of ourselves now becomes a painful process.

It may even be so painful, we may be resonating so far out of sync with the Whole, that re-integration no longer becomes possible. And then our little energy wave-form is doomed to bounce around the Universe for all time utterly alone - or at best only able to connect with other wave forms that are as wretched and hateful as we are.

This is Hell – not a curse but a warning that if we don't recognize our essential oneness we are doomed to never experience it. We are all facets of a hyper-dimensional crystal, each reflecting an aspect of the divine (see chapter 3). Experiencing the crystal is Heaven.

Chapter 21 - Waking in the Dream

On a couple of occasions in my life I have had lucid dreams. In one such dream, I had to get up and go somewhere. I was walking to whatever my destination was when I noticed that it was suddenly quite dark out and I realized that I should have still been home in bed.

I also noticed that I hadn't remembered to get dressed, but I still had my blanket with me. I tied my blanket over my shoulder and around me like a toga and started heading back home. As I walked, I met up with a friend of mine, and we started walking together. But my friend wanted to stop in a grocery store we were passing by to get a cup of coffee.

While in the store something odd happened - I can't quite remember what it was, but it was no odder than it suddenly becoming dark out or finding myself on the street naked. But whatever it was, I remember thinking this time "that can't be right, that's really weird, I must be dreaming". And then, as I thought about it, I realized that I truly was dreaming, and that this was a great opportunity to explore dreaming consciously.

First I looked around to see if I could tell the difference between the dream world and the "real" world, and was amazed at how "real" everything seemed. I touched the counters and they felt like counters. I smelled the produce and it smelled like produce. I looked carefully at everything around me and it all looked absolutely real. And yet, I was still convinced that I was dreaming.

Then I decided to try to do something impossible. I found some toothpicks on the counter and took one, thinking that if this was a dream I should be able to poke it through my hand. But when I tried it - ouch! It hurt! But how could it? The toothpick wasn't real. It was just something I was imagining.

Then I tried poking my finger through the palm of my other hand – still no success. My hand was as solid as if it was a real hand. I woke up before I could try any other experiments.

In my next and only other lucid dream, I once again tried to experiment within the dream, with only very little success at consciously altering the reality of the dream world. It has made me wonder. Here I have created a dream world out of my psyche and, since it is entirely my creation, I would expect that I should be able to alter the physical laws of that "reality" and have absolute power over my creation.

And yet I have found that even though I knew that everyone and everything I was experiencing in my dream was fabricated out of my mind, I could only interact with things in my dream as though they were actually outside of my body and not a part of me.

Although I have heard that other people who have had lucid dreams often do consciously manipulate their experience, my personal experience, to date, has been that within this created dream world I am powerless (at least so far) to consciously make anything happen that I wouldn't expect to happen in my day-to-day experiential reality.

How is not being able to "do the impossible" in my dream world any different from not being able to "do the impossible" in my waking world? And if there is no difference, do I indeed have just as much power to "do the impossible" in the "real" world, if only, as in the dream world, I could just figure out how?

The next time I have a lucid dream, I hope to interact with other people in my dream, and say to them "I know that you are actually a part of my own subconscious. Why have you appeared to me in this dream and what do you have to tell me." I think it may be interesting to hear what they say.

The waking world, though, shouldn't be all that different. We can only perceive a tiny fraction of the information coming into our senses about the world around us. We extrapolate what the world is really like from that limited information. This is like taking a trip all the way around the Earth and only being aware of a few hundred feet of the journey.

Extrapolating what the entire world is really like from that short walk is obviously going to be inherently inaccurate. A huge amount of information gets filtered out, and the tiny amount that we do process gets through only because our subconscious filters allow it to.

So in the waking world what we experience is in many ways really only a reflection of our subconscious.

What this means is that we are dreaming in the waking world nearly as much as we are when we dream while asleep. The people we draw into our lives, every interaction we experience, says more about our own subconscious than it does about the "real world".

How much more interesting everyone we meet becomes when we think of them as parts of our subconscious with a message for us!

Chapter 22 - Getting To Know Yourself

When our awareness is deep within whatever mental state we happen to be in, we end up being at the mercy of the neural network that defines that state. When we can rise above that state and be in our observer state, we have the ability to choose whether to get caught up in the story or to recognize the story for what it is. This is an important part of the pathway to becoming conscious.

When we are unconscious and dreaming, the "world" we experience in our dream is a creation of our own subconscious that appears to have substance outside of us but in reality is being created by neural networks firing within our brain. As long as we react to those self-generated images in our dream as though they were real, we will remain trapped in an illusion and won't realize that we are in fact unconscious, at least until the alarm clock goes off.

In the waking world, we tend to believe that what we perceive around us as "reality" has an existence independent of ourselves, and exists pretty much as we perceive it, whether we are there to perceive it or not. The fact is, though, that we are only able to be aware of a tiny fraction of the external world, and the tiny portion we can see is determined by our subconscious filters and triggers.

The more we understand these filters and triggers, the more we are able to rise above them and see a clearer view of the world that is more representative of the true situation and less of our personal baggage. This is The Work, and is a vital part of the process of waking up.

Though it is vital, The Work is not easy, and in fact often feels uncomfortable, especially in the beginning of the journey. But I have found pleasure and fulfillment in things I once found uncomfortable. I have done this by getting to know fully that which makes me uncomfortable, and learning to balance the positive I find with the negative I once thought was all there was.

You can't get to know the uncomfortable if you run away from it.

When we find ourselves saying something like "I'm drawn to X, but I would never go down that road so far as to Y", then most likely, "Y" is exactly the one place you really need to go.

To grow, we have to shift our thinking. The really big growth opportunities require paradigm shifts. It's scary to change your thinking, and the closer you get to what you need to be shifting into, the scarier it gets. The draw is there as well.

On some deep level we recognize that that is why we are here and we feel the draw, but as we get closer, the fear overwhelms the draw and makes it difficult to reach the goal. The fear, however, drops off faster than the draw, so there is a region where the draw is stronger than the fear. But there is still enough fear present that it makes our adrenal glands give a squirt and we feel the excitement - the draw spiced up with a zing of adrenaline.

This then is how the system is supposed to work. We are drawn to something. As we test the waters, it feels exciting and wonderful and fulfilling. Now we know we are on the right path!

As we continue to explore, we get used to whatever it was that was a little scary, and the fear diminishes. Now we can go further, closer to the goal. And in fact we must in order to feel that adrenaline rush of excitement. Eventually this too becomes tame, and we move closer still.

At some point the fear is reduced to the point that it no longer blocks us from reaching the end point, and we are able to make the paradigm shift without trauma. We can reach the goal and find that the fear that held us back is no longer there.

Go where you fear to go and fear will go.

The system can break down in one of two ways: going too fast, and going too slow. Pushing ourselves to grow faster than we are ready is traumatic and needlessly unpleasant. At the same time, it is all too easy to become complacent in the known, to find comfort in routine and safety.

But at the slower end of the spectrum we find ourselves sleepwalking through life, filling our hours with television and other meaningless drivel, until one day we find ourselves old and wondering how it happened. Our experience isn't always dull in this dulled state, though, as life will keep throwing stuff at us to deal with in an attempt to wake us up and get us moving along the path.

So this is how we tell if we're on the right track. Is life too dull? Too traumatic? Then something is wrong. Is life exciting and fulfilling, with challenges that are easily met? Then things are right where they need to be.

Chapter 23 - Ecstatic Dance

There are many tools available to us to use in the exploration of those deeper hidden parts of ourselves. One of the most useful for me on my own journey has been Ecstatic Dance. Ecstatic Dance is a dynamic meditation, guided by the use of specific beats and rhythms (often utilizing the 5 Rhythms format developed by Gabrielle Roth) to lead the dancer on an inner journey to connect with Source and invite healing.

Ecstatic dance is about moving in whatever way is authentic for you in the moment. Generally that looks like, well, dancing, but can also be expressed in other ways such as rolling on the floor and drooling, moving in a sexual/sensual manner, meditating quietly or weeping loudly. Space is held for all forms of expression without judgment. The only "rules" really are no conversations on the dance floor, and be open to letting people have their own experience.

Long ago, when tribal people danced, it wasn't with precisely learned steps but rather the music or drumming moved the dancers to dance ecstatically. As humans became more "civilized", rules were made and had to be followed. Dance became a performance.

Dance started to regain some of its ecstatic nature with the advent of rock and roll. The hippies of the sixties promoted "do your own thing", and this was reflected in the music of the day as people ignored the rules and started to dance in ways that just felt good. Nevertheless, there were still some restrictions when dancing to rock-and-roll. You may have been doing your own thing, but you were still doing it to the music, still trying to look good.

Ecstatic dance takes it another level up and returns to what was lost in our tribal roots. With ecstatic dance, it's not about looking good. It's about "dance ugly and drool". It's about being so deeply into the dance that you're only aware of others as some vague vibrations while your movements are guided by what's deep within instead of by what your conscious mind thinks would look good.

There have been other examples throughout history of regaining our tribal roots in dance. One of the more interesting was a supposed medical condition, common in the 16th and 17th centuries in southern Italy, called tarantism. Tarantism was presumed to be caused by the bite of a tarantula (or more likely a type of wolf spider as true tarantulas don't actually live in southern Italy). And for some reason, young women seemed to be particularly susceptible to being bitten.

Once envenomated, the only cure was to dance wildly until the toxin was sweated out of the body. When it became known that a victim had been bitten, the townspeople would grab their musical instruments and start playing the frantic music, helping the poor girl to fall under the spell of the music and dance out the venom and thus save her life.

Supposedly a particular kind of dance, called the tarentella, evolved from this therapy, but at its roots this was an ecstatic dance and often included ripping off one's clothing and dancing naked in the frenzied dancing delirium. It is now known that no spiders were ever actually to blame for this condition. Rather, the guise of emergency therapy for bite victims was likely the only socially acceptable outlet for wild ecstatic dancing in an increasingly suppressive culture.

The trouble was that you only got to express yourself in this way once or at best a few times in your life. If it became more frequent than that, you would likely arouse suspicion that just maybe you actually enjoyed this sort of thing. And there would go your reputation.

Those who provide music for ecstatic dance often will use a series of specific rhythms to enhance the dance experience, the most common being the 5 Rhythms discovered and developed by Gabrielle

Roth. These rhythms consist of Flow, Staccato, Chaos, Lyrical and Stillness, a cycle of all of these in that order constituting a Wave.

It is not necessary for the dancer to be aware of the 5 Rhythms to have a deep dance experience. But those who seek the deeper experiences tend to gravitate towards those who provide those waves since that's what tends to provide the deep experiences they are looking for.

So what exactly are these deep experiences found in this form of dance? They will, of course, vary from dance to dance and individual to individual. Letting the mind follow the body rather than the body following the mind will often lead to awareness of body memories and allow access to the non-verbal portions of ourselves.

For myself, ecstatic dance is a way of communing with Spirit, and such communing brings about insights and shows me answers to deep questions. In fact, many of the chapters of this book are a direct result of insights gleaned from ecstatic dance. Here are some examples I have received from ecstatic dance, taken from my journal of insights:

Dancing Fear, Dancing Pain

This week's invitation at dance was to dance our fears. As I danced I started thinking about scary movies, about how we enjoy being scared as long as it's safe, and what makes scary movies safe is that: A) it's Hollywood and we know that the writers will make it all turn out good in the end (unless it's not Hollywood but some indie film based on some Russian play or something, but who wants to watch that?) and B) we are disassociated from the fear, watching it play out before us but not in the middle of it.

So, when we are experiencing fear in our lives, all we need to do is trust that if we make the best decisions we can in any given moment, it will all work out for the best in the end, to trust in The Writer. Also, step back from the fear, disassociate yourself from it and it will have less power over you.

The other thing that came up for me during dance was the importance of being in the moment. This again related to the intention in that in general most of our fears have little to do with what's happening in the moment but instead with worrying about what will happen in the future based on what has happened in the past.

It's seldom true that the lion is actually chasing us right now. It's like the story of the optimist who fell off a skyscraper, and was heard to say as he passed the 10th floor... "So far, so good". If there's nothing you can do about it anyway, why not enjoy the fall?

Last Sunday my wife Sam gave the intention for Sacred Circle Dance, which included being grateful for and listening to the different parts of our bodies. The body part that first grabbed my attention was my lower back and hip that was feeling pain.

Pain generally demands to be attended to first, so I danced to those body parts that were painful. But I found that I just got stuck there, and the pain was getting worse. Eventually I started paying attention more to what felt good, not what felt bad, and by the end of dance the painful parts were hardly painful at all. It goes to show that whatever we put energy into will grow.

Dancing Into Openness, Evolving Into Something Greater.

This time the invitation for dance was to start with self-massage, self-appreciation and love, and as the dance went on to gradually open up to interacting with, massaging and appreciating others.

As I danced, what came to me was how all throughout the history of the evolution of the universe, there has been a pattern of losing autonomy in order to create a higher order (see chapter 8).

Subatomic particles came together, losing their autonomy and became trapped in a diverse array of atoms. Atoms lost their autonomy but in return became integral parts of more complex molecules. Single celled organisms gave up their autonomy, became specialized for specific jobs as part of greater multi-cellular organisms with vastly more potential.

Each evolutionary quantum leap brought with it a vastly increased potential for complexity and power, and came about by opening up to resonating and integrating with others, other particles, other atoms, other cells, to create something entirely new.

As I danced, and in my dance went from being closed up deep within myself to opening to being part of a more complex dance involving all the other dancers, I felt as though I was recapitulating the evolution of the universe. And I felt as though we were all on the cusp of something greater, nearly ready to transform from selfish individuals into parts of a greater whole, something greater than anything we could ever imagine.

And just as a nerve cell has no concept of what it means to be a brain but only "knows" that it is a cell within the organism that likes to pass on electrical pulses, I knew I could have no concept of what exactly it is that we are becoming. Only that whatever it is, I wanted to be the organism within this hyper-organism that liked to have fun and love unconditionally. However being that serves the greater hyper-organism, that is my role and my destiny.

Dancing Your Own Dance, Dancing Another's

The invitation at Dance this week was to find the balance between dancing someone else's dance and finding your own dance.

What came up for me was "What do you do when dancing someone else's dance is incompatible with dancing your own?"

When this happens, I feel frustrated, trapped and controlled by external influences, even though I recognize that I am trapped in a prison of my own construction (i.e. it is only my own attachment to continuing to dance another's dance that keeps me from dancing my own).

I danced with this feeling of being forced by external influences into living a life that wasn't satisfying to me, and after a while pondered what the opposite would look like. What I came up with was the affirmation "everything goes my way".

What I realized was that if everything went my way, it wouldn't matter whether I was being controlled by external influences or securely in control of my own destiny - either way things would be going my way, and would make the question of whether or not I was actually being controlled a moot point.

At that point I decided to try a reality shift, using this new affirmation as the guide. I knew I could achieve the greatest and most permanent shift if I coupled it with an ego death, at least a little one, so I slipped out and got a lung full of nitrous oxide, then came back to dance "everything goes my way". Another dancer interrupted me to ask if I was all right, but despite that it felt at least partially successful; how long it lasts remains to be seen.

Sam's dance revealed feelings of being used when dancing someone else's dance - that they only cared about their own dance and not hers. It reminded her of times in her life when others wanted to take from her sexually without seeming to care for her.

Again, this was created in her own psyche. It may or may not have been true that they didn't care about her. But it doesn't really matter; it is only the feeling that she was used that scarred her, and that feeling came from within herself.

If she felt cared for by all of those people, it wouldn't really matter whether it was "true" or not, and for all she knows they all did care about her, at least to some degree. I suggested the affirmation "I am cared for", and a reality shift using that as a guide.

Philosophical thoughts and insights are not the only benefit I get from ecstatic dance. Being a type of meditation, ecstatic dance naturally puts me into the observer state, from which I can notice my thought processes without getting caught up in them (see chapter 24).

For example, I used to have a particular troublesome thought come up for me at times when I was dancing with another person. For some reason I would get it in my head that the person I was dancing with was probably ready to move on. Some part of my subconscious tried to talk me into believing that the other person was only still dancing with me because they didn't know how to break away, perhaps because they didn't want to hurt my feelings.

I then would break off the dance, trying to take care of them by offering them an "out". Even if I was enjoying the connection immensely, I would end up cutting it short all because of a stupid story I had made up in my head for which there was absolutely no hard evidence.

But the dance naturally helps put you into the observer state, and from that vantage point I could more clearly see what I was doing, the motivations behind why I was doing it, and how silly the whole thing was.

And then I could choose a different way. I could decide that even if they really were looking to be done with dancing with me, I wasn't under any obligation to make that happen for them. I could choose to trust that they would break off the dance when they were ready to.

And then I found that my dances would last a lot longer, sometimes to the point where I had had enough and broke it off, sometimes until they had had enough and broke it off, but always until it was at a more authentic time to do so rather than because some stupid story in my head told me to.

The experiences above are merely examples of the sort of way I benefit from dance, but other people experience other things. Though individual results may vary, generally most people who get into ecstatic dance find that it becomes a practice that helps them heal old trauma, rewrite old stories, and grow more conscious.

The Shadow

Often in dance there will be an intention to dance the shadow, or some specific aspect of our shadow. The shadow is the parts of ourselves that we don't want to look at, that we relegate to our subconscious so that our conscious doesn't have to be aware of it. But if we don't deal with the things we relegate to our subconscious, we end up manifesting them in our outside reality and deal with them there, where it is generally a less pleasant experience (see chapters 15 and 21). It's better to be consciously aware of our shadow, and transform it by shining a light into it.

I used to be reluctant to connect with my shadow; it seemed a scary place to go. Over time I learned the value in getting to know our dark places, at first more as a necessary evil than a pleasant experience, and eventually to appreciate and enjoy shadow work.

Gabrielle Roth speaks to the transformation that can happen when you dance your shadow. In her book *Sweat Your Prayers - the 5 Rhythms of the Soul*, she writes:

> *"Just as an alchemist spins dross into gold, by dancing the dark we transform it to light. Negative energy and suffering become mere grist for the mill. In the dance, we discover parts of us we've cast in the shadows and by bringing them into the light we diffuse their power over us. In the shadows mother is smothering and devouring. Mistress is numb, pissed off, and depressed. Madonna is manipulative and obsessive. Father is overbearing and rigid. Son is destructive, aimless, and uncommunicative. Holy Spirit is judgmental and dogmatic. In the shadows the artist is an imitator and a predator who relies on the creativity of others. The lover is abusive and frigid. And the seeker, of course, founds a commune and becomes a guru."*

Further on in the chapter Gabrielle Roth writes:

> *"Then I got up and started dancing – I didn't even bother with music. Instead of being*

afraid of the empty hole I dove right into it. I thought to myself, Alice did it – why can't I? I danced and I danced until the hole became holy, until the emptiness became sacred space."

I remember one particular dance that was focused on shadow work. During the dance I found myself rolling around on the floor with my wife, Sam, exchanging energy and juiciness. But then I thought that this didn't seem very shadowy, so I started to consider what the shadow is in my perception of Sam.

The first thing that popped into my mind was how I get irritated when Sam and I are going out and she has to try on six different outfits, as though they somehow will look different on her this time. I thought about how I get so frustrated that I finally just wish she'd put on anything just so we could get going.

And I found that rolling around on the floor with her and feeling the juiciness and the frustration at the same time helped to transform how I saw those things that irritated me, and her fashion indecision became an endearing quality rather than a source of frustration. Shining the light of the juiciness into the shadow transformed it into something pleasant.

Then I started doing the same thing with other dark places in my psyche. I thought of some of the fights Sam and I have had, and some things Sam has said to me during those times that hurt me to my core. And again I was able to transform my perception. I was able to compassionately see Sam saying these hurtful things as someone who was acting out of a painful place and not take her words personally.

Next, I took on the issues I have with my mother and how judgmental she can be. Again I was able to transform my perspective and see her as someone who was so insecure with herself that she had to judge others in order to not have to see her own inadequacies. And again I was able to not take her words personally.

These transformations happened effortlessly, simply by dancing with intention. I discovered during that dance that shadow work doesn't have to be unpleasant at all.

These sorts of insights don't always stop you from reacting to things that trigger you each and every time they come up from that day forth. But each time we achieve such a perspective, it lays down and reinforces new neural pathways which make seeing things from that perspective easier the next time such things come up.

Chapter 24 - Meditation

Meditation has historically been one of the most common tools for gaining self-knowledge and raising consciousness. Though I personally tend to get more benefit out of the more dynamic meditation of ecstatic dance (see chapter 23), the traditional sitting still and quieting the mind kind of meditation has been a mainstay on the consciousness pathway.

I am by no means an expert on meditation, but I believe that the purpose of meditation is to put the meditator into the observer state, a state of simple awareness. Some visual experiences I have had while in altered brain states have helped me to see what happens to our consciousness in this state and why being in such a state is so important.

I have participated in several ayahuasca ceremonies over the years. Ayahuasca is made from a combination of herbs indigenous to South America and utilized by shamans to help guide participants in healing spiritual journeys.

Ayahuasca produces its effects by releasing DMT (Dimethyltryptamine) into the nervous system. DMT is a neurotransmitter/neuromodulator produced naturally in the human brain and is involved in certain psychological and neurological states. J. C. Callaway, a medical researcher, suggested in 1988 that DMT might be connected with visual dream phenomena (Callaway J (1988). "A proposed mechanism for the visions of dream sleep". Med Hypotheses26 (2): 119–24. doi:10.1016/0306-9877(88)90064-3. PMID 3412201.).

Another researcher, J.V. Wallach, proposed a new hypothesis that in addition to being involved in altered states of consciousness, DMT produced in the brain may be involved in the creation of normal waking states of consciousness by acting as a neurotransmitter at "trace amine" receptors in the brain. Wallach proposes that in this way waking consciousness can be thought of as a controlled psychedelic experience. (Wallach J.V. (January 2009). "Endogenous hallucinogens as ligands of the trace amine receptors: a possible role in sensory perception". *Medical Hypotheses* **72** (1): 91-4.doi:10.1016/j.mehy.2008.07.052. PMID 18805646)

Yet another researcher, Dr. Rick Strassman, while conducting DMT research in the 1990s at the University of New Mexico, advanced the controversial hypothesis that a massive release of DMT from the pineal gland prior to death or near death was the cause of the near death experience (NDE) phenomenon. (Strassman, Rick J. (2001). *DMT: The Spirit Molecule. A Doctor's Revolutionary Research into the Biology of Near-Death and Mystical Experiences*. Rochester, Vt: Park Street.ISBN 978-0-89281-927-0. ("Chapter summaries". Retrieved 27 February 2012.))

All of this suggests that DMT is a molecule that may be central to the exploration of consciousness, and why natural sources of DMT such as ayahuasca are so useful in shamanic ceremonies.

I have had some amazing and life-changing experiences during my ayahuasca journeys. Each experience has been unique. Some experiences have been disappointingly uneventful, while others have brought joyous enlightenment or deep emotional struggle. Some have brought me amazing visual experiences, while other times I won't see anything but will feel things happening in my body.

Ayahuasca has a reputation for causing "purging", or vomiting, which is why I often refer to it as "the hurl and whirl"; generally the purging is mild and not unpleasant though I have had some times when I thought I was about to vomit up half of my internal organs. But just as frequently I will go through the entire evening without physically purging even once.

It is the visual experiences I wish to talk about here. When I have had visual experiences on ayahuasca they often have been similar to what other people have seen. I will see patterns painted with lines of energy, usually in a fluorescent green or green and deep purple. The energy lines will sometimes form patterns that some have described as "sacred geometry".

They are usually beautiful to look at, but when I try to look closely to remember the details they will usually fade away. Unfortunately I am not an artist, for I would dearly love to bring back examples of what I have seen and do them justice on a canvas. The works of the artist Alex Gray is often reminiscent of some of the things I have seen, and I envy his ability to reproduce some of these images (although I remember after one intensely visual journey I came away thinking that Alex Gray really lacked imagination).

There is one pattern, though, that I have been able to remember enough to try to reproduce. One of the things I have seen is a pattern of roundish irregular blotches or patches that remind me of the patterns on the shells of tortoises, except the blotches are made of concentric lines of energy. It is interesting that in Chinese lore the tortoise is said to carry the pattern of all existence on his back. At times I have seen a flat field of these patterns, and to the best of my ability to reproduce them, they look something like this:

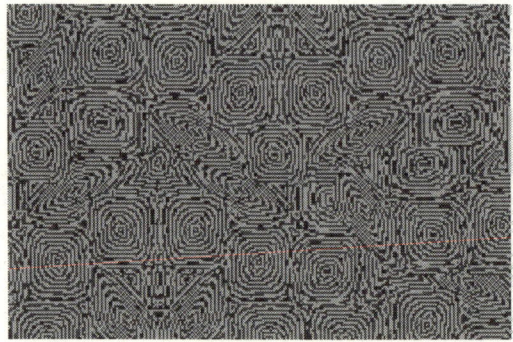

But other times I will see a sort of egg shaped energy structure. This Egg is covered with the same pattern of roundish irregular blotches or patches, and looks something like this:

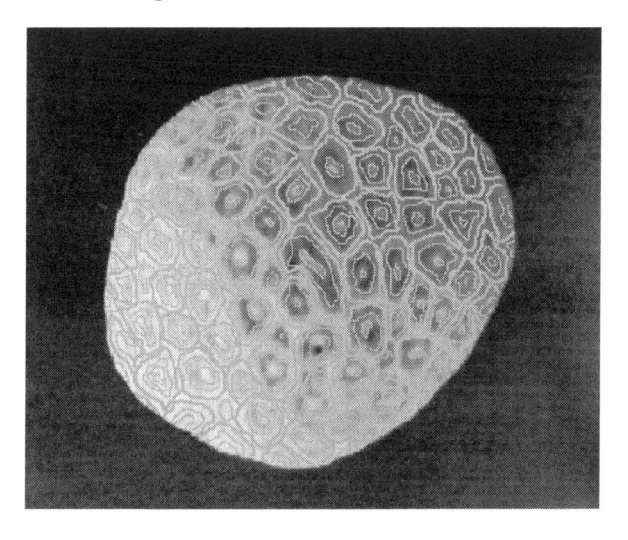

And sometimes, I will see the Egg sitting on or perhaps being an out-pocketing of the field, looking something like this:

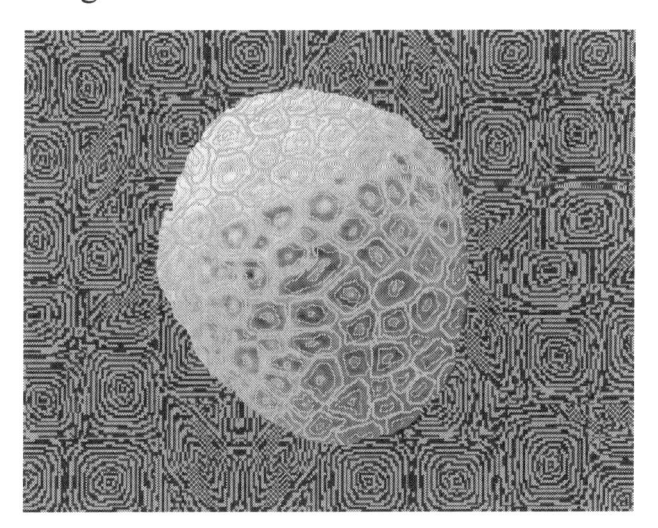

Now, the interesting thing is that when I put my attention on any one of those little swirls covering the Egg, it will suddenly expand until I suddenly find myself inside a tunnel of energy lines, extending away to infinity. It looks something like this:

When I'm in the tunnel, it becomes my entire experience, and I find it difficult to even remember that I was just looking at the Egg. I just fly down the tunnel, which keeps expanding infinitely like a fractal zoom (see chapter 36).

With some effort, if I can remember to do so, I can pull myself back up out of the tunnel and see the overview of the Egg again. But if I attach to, or put attention on, any other swirl, the vortex opens up once again and I am back in a new tunnel.

I have come to believe that the pattern of whirls on the egg is a visual representation of the pluripotential field of all possible realities, and/or all the possible conscious states I could be in (which is really the same thing, since reality is determined by consciousness), as seen from my observer state. When I looked at any one whirl, I was collapsing the wave-form into one state which became everything and I was no longer able to be aware of the other potential whirls/states/realities I could be in.

This visual and the way I am interpreting it has helped me be aware of the importance of being in one's observer state and how being there helps keep you from getting caught up in any one story. Or it can give you the power to consciously choose which story to get caught up in if that's what you choose to do.

It has also shown me the importance of not attaching. When you attach to any one particular whirl (by putting attention on it), then you fall in, and it becomes everything.

The secret to staying centered, spacious and not caught up in triggers is to stay above it all and not attach to any one story. If you don't like the way things are playing out in your life, realize that what's playing out is just one story, just one of the whirls you have gotten attached to.

Detach from that story by getting into the observer state, where you can see all of the stories, and from there choose a better story to attach to (or better yet, if you can, don't attach to any at all).

What all this has to do with meditation is that meditation puts you into the observer state, a state of simple awareness that avoids getting caught up in stories about what you are aware of. The internal chatter of the mind is one of the swirls on the egg, and paying attention to the chatter causes you to fall into its spell and get caught up in the chatter.

During meditation, the chatter is quieted, and any thoughts that do come up are simply observed and allowed to pass on by, which allows the meditator to not get caught up in them. Observing your breathing and observing your thoughts puts you into the observer state, which I believe is the whole point of meditation.

This observer state can also be achieved in other ways, such as in dance (see chapter 23). When you are being danced by the music, you are no longer doing the dancing. You can enter a state where you are watching your body move to the music but not consciously guiding the movements; this is again the observer state.

The more we reside in the observer state through meditation (or through dance or some of the exercises I will describe in chapter 25), the more we can avoid getting caught up in stories and have more freedom to choose consciously how our life will unfold (see chapter 4).

During the moving meditation that is ecstatic dance, I have often been advised to "follow where your feet want to go" or "notice how your hands want to move". It took me a long time to really get what the facilitator was getting at. I would try to feel into where or how my hands or feet wanted to move, and then when I thought I knew, I, or my ego, would move them that way.

But it wasn't my hands or feet that was doing the moving, it was my ego back in the driver's seat. It took me a while to realize that I just needed to let my hands or feet do what they wanted to do while my ego just needed to be the observer.

Following your breath is a good way to practice being in the observer state, because the breath lives in both worlds: the controlled as well as the autonomic. When we aren't thinking about it, we breathe just fine. But we also can control very easily just how fast or deep we are breathing (unless we breathe so slowly or shallowly that after a while we get oxygen depleted, and then our autonomic system steps in).

In fact, we control the breath so easily that we often tend to start taking control over at least part of the rate and depth of our breath as soon as our attention is brought to our breath. We may be observing our breathing, but our ego easily slips into the driver's seat even as we observe our breath. It is good to practice simply observing our breath without in any way influencing it. Once you have that down, you can expand that observation mode to include observing your hands or feet during dance, and eventually to your life in general.

The ego seems to think it has to control everything, when in fact there are very good subconscious subroutines in place that can handle most of our daily activities with the ease they handle breathing. Our egos really only just need to observe, and only step in when the situation really calls for it, which is a lot rarer than our egos believe it to be.

Our egos are like a little kid in the passenger seat with a fake steering wheel. Both the ego and the kid think they are doing the driving, both think they are doing a pretty good job of it, when in fact it is our subconscious that is really doing the work over in the driver's seat. The ego does have an important role, but it also has an over-important sense of itself and thinks it has more of a role than it really does.

I have had the experience, while meditating on mushrooms, of getting into an observer state, and then observing myself in the observer state, and then observing myself observing myself in the observer state, and so on until I was stepping back in observation levels in groups of 5, 10, 20, more and more layers upon layers, until I got to about 250 layers of observation. At that point I was able to basically grab all of the rest of the layers, all the way to infinity, and arrived at a state where I was no longer I. There were no more layers to observe from. I experienced ego death, and, in that moment, oneness with everything.

Each layer that you can observe from carries with it a certain flavor of consciousness. When you start observing yourself, you become aware of your actions, the effects that they have, your triggers, things that tend to make us move one way or another. We become aware of these things and realize that we have an obligation to make the right choice, because karma will reflect our choices back to us.

But when we go to the next layer, observing ourselves as the observer (being conscious of being conscious - see chapter 8), we reach a new flavor of consciousness, the perspective that the choices and decisions we make really don't matter that much. We realize that we are simply part of a whole tapestry and that each thread, whatever twists and turns it makes along the way, is beautiful and perfect just as it is.

The whole is a holographic reflection of each individual part. If the whole is beautiful, then all the parts that make it up are also beautiful. When we reach this stage of reflection, where that's how we view creation, we realize that we don't really need to struggle, to try so much.

So the first rung of the ladder is becoming conscious of awareness of our responsibility of our actions, while the next rung of the ladder is becoming aware that it's all beautiful and perfect, and the whole reflects perfectly who we are.

The third rung of the ladder brings us back into responsibility, but in a different way. Scientists at the Max Planck Institute for Human Cognitive and Brain Sciences have conducted experiments utilizing fMRI that show that our decisions are made a full seven seconds before we become aware of making a decision (see Keim, Brandon (April 13, 2008). "Brain Scanners Can See Your Decisions Before You Make Them". *Wired News*(CondéNet), and Chun Siong Soon, Marcel Brass, Hans-Jochen Heinze, John-Dylan Haynes (April 13, 2008). "Unconscious determinants of free decisions in the human brain (Abstract)". *Nature*

Neuroscience(Nature Publishing Group) **11** (5): 543–5.doi:10.1038/nn.2112. PMID 18408715, and http://exploringthemind.com/the-mind/brain-scans-can-reveal-your-decisions-7-seconds-before-you-decide).

Patterns can be seen on the fMRI that show whether we will, for example, push a button on the left or push a button on the right up to seven seconds before we are aware that we are about to make a decision. It seems that any decision we make consciously has already been made previously on a subconscious level. What is likely to be going on here is that when we consciously know that we will need to make a decision, we subconsciously start to decide how we are going to handle that decide in anticipation of making a conscious decision in the near future, and delegate that decision to a decision-making subroutine in our subconscious.

This decision-making subroutine makes the decision and then sends back the information to our consciousness whereupon we then think that we are making the decision in that moment of time, when in actuality our subroutine made it for us moments ago. So it doesn't really matter what "we" (our conscious egos) decide, our subroutines have already decided for us.

It would be interesting to set up an experiment where we are told from the fMRI scan what our decision is going to be between, say, picking the left square or the right square on a video screen, and then deciding to choose the opposite. I suspect though that that decision to go one way and then suddenly go another, is also decided in our subconscious; that too would be predicted that that would be what we would decide in that moment.

All of this shows that whatever decisions we make actually are fine, they have already been made by a wiser decision-making subroutine. That's what we use to make our decisions and that's already happened before we even decide that we need to decide. So what becomes important on this third rung of the ladder is not what we decide, but what question to ask.

For example, if the question we want to make a decision about concerns choosing between two things that are both beneficial or desirable, then it doesn't really matter all that much which way our decision making subroutine goes. We end up winning either way.

On the other hand, if the choice we send to our decision-making subroutine is between, say, something unpleasant and something pleasant yet ultimately hurtful to somebody else (the "stuck between a rock and a hard place" dilemma), then our subroutine is bound to send back a bad decision one way or the other.

It is important to be open to all the choices, consider all the actions we can take as long as they are actions that support the greater good, and not put up for consideration those choices that are harmful. If you're stuck between a rock and a hard place, look for a solution that lies in a different direction from either the rock or the hard place. Those choices may require thinking outside of the box.

Life may be carrying us along like a river, and sometimes it may feel like a river of toxic sludge, and it may feel like our only choices are to either continue on downstream or to fight the current and swim upstream, but either way we are still in the toxic river. We get stuck in what seems like limited choices and forget that we might instead, for example, get out of the river onto a sandy beach or, if there is no beach, scale up the sides of the canyon wall - a difficult path but one that leads to a satisfying solution.

The point is to be open to all of the possible alternatives, even the difficult ones, and send our decision-making subroutines only those choices that are neither rocks nor hard places.

Chapter 25 - Getting Into Your Observer State

Our different states of being are all just neural networks that we shift into and can just as easily shift out of. We can even learn to do this shift purposefully. The key is to not get caught up in those energy tunnels that trap you in a story (see chapter 24). Instead, shift your observer state and notice from that higher perspective what your state of mind is, feel how it feels, and understand where it's coming from.

From there you can choose a different perspective and see if that changes how you feel about your situation. We can choose perspectives that shift our state of being, but only if we don't believe everything we feel (see chapter 4).

There are many ways to shift your consciousness into a state of observation and simple awareness. In addition to Dance and Meditation (see chapters 23 and 24), there are some exercises that can also help put you there.

One way to practice putting yourself into observer mode is to get into the habit of from time to time asking yourself "what am I doing?" By simply observing yourself doing whatever it is you are doing in that moment, you will automatically pop out of being caught up in whatever you are doing and become the observer.

It is generally true that the reality of an anticipated event or experience is quite different from what we expected it to feel like. Whether it is a vacation to some special part of the world, the lifestyle we imagine we'll have when we win the lottery, or the ménage a trois with the hot twins at work, the actual experience is typically quite different from what we thought it would be.

If you find yourself experiencing something that you have been anticipating, try to remember how you thought it would feel, and compare that to the actual experience. Contrasting the actual experience with the anticipated experience helps us to really feel into the experience, notice more fully what it really feels like, and be more in the moment. Saying to yourself "oh, this is what this experience feels like" is one trick to help bring us more fully into the Now and shift into the observer state.

Another way to put yourself into observer mode is to pretend that you are in a virtual reality story about yourself. Imagine that some advanced civilization develops such a good virtual reality interface that the user would have no way to tell the difference between the virtual reality experience and what we believe is the real reality experience.

This theoretical exceptionally realistic virtual reality experience is so complete that it even provides the user with childhood memories and built-in emotional triggers. It would provide everything that would be needed to totally experience what it's like not only to live and interact in a certain setting, but also to feel the feelings, think the thoughts, react to the triggers, and in every other possible way to experience being another person.

If one chose, one could pick from a huge library of different lives that one could experience. A long-lived alien race could choose to download and experience your entire lifetime in the same way that you or I might choose to watch a 2 hour movie. Or a shorter-lived race might download and experience a 2 year or 2 hour or 2 minute significant moment from your lifetime, complete with all the memories that lead up to that moment.

Of course, to be a truly authentic experience, the user would have to have their memories of who they really are temporarily suppressed during the experience. You don't experience your actual life with any other memories other than your own, so you wouldn't want them in the virtual experience of your life either.

It wouldn't need to be an actual person's life that was downloaded to experience; it could be a fictional story written in intricate detail. While experiencing the story, the user would never realize that the whole story was already written out, and all the decisions they struggled over had already been decided by the Writer. Just as when reading a book about a character who might struggle with some decision, you could experience their struggle as you "read" along, or skip a few "pages" ahead and see what they ended up deciding, or even replay the same passage over and over to keep re-experiencing the struggle if you chose to.

The virtual reality experiencer, however, having forgotten that it's all just a story, would be too caught up in the story to remember that it's all just a story and they're just in the equivalent of a theater.

This scenario may be entirely possible at some point in the future, perhaps the very near future given the accelerating pace of technology and advancements in virtual reality systems. Just as today we pay a fee to watch a movie, someday soon we may be able to go someplace, pay a fee, and experience what it was like to be another person for a period of time.

From time to time as you go about your day, pretend that you are actually somebody else who has purchased a ride through this segment of your life (maybe because it was a fun experience or may because you are really a anthropologist from the far future experiencing what everyday life was like for people like you). Imagine that, with your "real" memories having been temporarily disabled, you are experiencing your life as though you were watching a virtual reality movie, curious about what you might do next, watching for plot twists, and just noting what it's like to be this person.

This is a good way to get yourself into the observer state while still carrying on with your daily activities. And it is from this observer state that we finally gain some control over our lives.

Of course, as far as you know, the virtual reality scenario may actually be true. You may really be from an advanced civilization with good virtual reality technology, experiencing a story of what it's like to be a human - specifically the human known as you (the "you" who is reading this right now), while the memories of the other "you" (the one taking the virtual reality ride) have been suppressed.

And if most of your life seems too boring to make an interesting story for someone to experience, just know that it's an art piece, and the boring bits are just part of the art and everything will come together in the end and all make some sort of sense. Or the story could just be a two or three hour clip of your life, for example the part where you read a book that helps you realize what's really going on and helps you wake up from the story.

When we live our lives stuck in the story, we get stuck in the reactions and triggers and emotions and drama and these things keep us from living intentionally. We end up having very little actual free will but instead our actions and decisions end up all being determined by our baggage and the events that happen to us (see chapter 9). Thus we think we have control, but we do not.

If we instead live our lives as though we are advanced beings experiencing a human story, we take a step back and become an observer of our life. We bought the ticket, now we're taking the ride, watching the drama from our safe and comfortable seat in the theater. And much like we can enjoy watching a scary movie from the safety of our theater seat, stepping back and observing our lives as though it was just a story unfolding before us allows us to experience scary moments in our lives from a position of relative safety and helps take the bite out of the fear.

The ironic thing is that it is only from that elevated position of observer that we actually do have any actual control over our lives.

Once we are no longer stuck in the story, we can find that we have a choice in how we react to the story and ultimately in how the story turns out. Thus, it is by giving up control and realizing that it's all just a story that has already been written that puts us in a position to actually write it.

Chapter 26 - An Example of Healing From the Observer State

Theory is all well and good, but there's nothing like real life examples to make a concept clear. I remember several years ago during a time in my life when my wife Sam and I were having a tumultuous period in our relationship, and my emotional state was tenuous at best. This was also a time in my life when I struggled with deep depression, and would from time to time sink into hopeless despair. And one day during this period I had an experience with being in the observer state that helped me turn a lot of this around.

It all started on Valentines' Day of 2009, but rather than the romantic time Sam and I were "supposed" to be having, we spent the day fighting and triggering each other, eventually missing a party we had been looking forward to attending. We did finally manage to reconnect later in the evening, but I was left rather emotionally raw. The next morning we headed out to our regular Sunday morning ecstatic dance.

On the way there I received a phone call from my friend Rusty, a woman who also tended to affect me on a deep emotional level. Rusty was extremely triggered about something that morning and proceeded to yell at me for 20 minutes, while I tried my best to hear her without taking it on. We got to dance very late, and it was a very difficult dance for me, with lots of hard emotions coming up.

Rusty showed up to dance as well about the same time Sam and I did, but wouldn't accept support from either Sam or myself. After dance Sam was feeling triggered by Rusty and we spent a long time walking around the city while I listened to and supported her. By the time we got home, I was feeling like an emotional toxic waste dump.

All the turmoil and struggle over the preceding 48 hours had taken their toll and I could no longer hold myself together and started slipping into a deep depression. I went off by myself to a private area in a corner of our property to cry, and fell deeper and deeper into hopeless despair. I couldn't stand it anymore, didn't want to do it anymore, just wanted to die and end the misery.

And then I suddenly found myself in my observer state, watching from the outside as I writhed in despair. From that perspective I was able to see that this miserable hopeless despairing state was just a part of me, a part that I visited from time to time but was no more and no less important than any other part. It was just a particularly sucky part to experience. It wasn't good or bad, it just was, and its existence was obviously doing something for me (or trying to do something for me) or I wouldn't visit there so frequently.

From that higher perspective I was able to have compassion for myself, for having this miserable part of me that so sucked to experience. I was able to mentally hold myself and say to myself "I'm so sorry you have this part within you, I know how much existence sucks for this part and I'm so sorry that you have to experience that misery." I could observe myself feeling comforted by my higher self, the part that was in the observer state, and could feel my lower self being suspended and supported by the compassion I was feeling for myself.

It became clear that the compassion I was feeling truly needed to be nonjudgmental or otherwise that unpleasant part of me would feel like my higher self was just trying to fix my lower self and not see that there might be something positive in the negative experience. Trying to fix it was akin to denying it, and denying it only makes it stronger.

After a while this desperate hopeless part of me started to say that if I was truly being nonjudgmental in my compassion, it would have to be able to fully express itself; it had to be able to say "no, you can't silence me" in order for it to also be able to say "OK, I can chose to be comforted and healed by my higher self's compassion."

And so that hopeless part of me became everything in order to accept that it could also become nothing.

I stopped breathing and had every intention of continuing to not breathe until I was dead, for that would be the ultimate expression of this horrible part of me. My consciousness though still resided in my higher self, and I continued to observe myself fall into utter despair, continued to watch dispassionately, nonjudgmentally, as my oxygen levels dropped, could observe me feeling my lungs crying out for air but, being "outside" that desperate need, was actually able to keep holding my breath far longer than I normally would have been able to.

I would feel myself starting to slip back into my body, start to be in the need to breathe again, and then remember to step back out and become the observer again, from where I could continue to not breathe. I watched myself start to slip away, and then suddenly I found myself breathing; I must have passed out briefly and my autonomic nervous system had taken over.

As I sat there breathing, I came back into my body and started feeling calm and serene. Apparently my body wanted to live, but I had for a moment given full voice to my despair. In doing so, I had allowed it to become healed by my compassion. If I hadn't been in my observer state, I never would have been able to have healed in this way.

Chapter 27 - Chemical Means of Exploring Consciousness

There are some short cuts on the pathway to expanded consciousness, through the use of psychedelics that alter our perspective, cut through our filters and expand our awareness. These shortcuts are not necessarily a good substitute for the longer routes such as meditation, but I believe that, used judiciously and with intention, temporary chemical enhancement can open doors that would otherwise take years to open and can serve to show us where it is possible to go on the consciousness pathway.

The goal is to eventually get there without the chemical support, but on the way there, the chemicals can act in a way to lift us up out of the fog so that we can feel what it is like to be enlightened and then set our bearings, so that when the chemicals wear off and we sink back into the fog, we can know what it is we are heading for.

Different chemicals can teach you different things, and some will take you down a path that looks appealing but actually leads away from the goal, so it is important to do your homework and chose your flavor of chemical assistance, if any, with wisdom. Many of these chemicals are currently illegal in many parts of the world, and one's willingness to risk the legal ramifications must also be factored into any decision to utilize these substances.

It is ludicrous that marijuana, psychedelics, amphetamines, barbiturates, narcotics and plants used in traditional shamanic ceremonies all get lumped together into the "drug" box, despite huge differences in toxicity, abuse potential, addictiveness, and beneficial effects. Many of these things have been given the "dangerous drug" label for reasons that have little to do with the actual toxicity or abuse potential of the substance so labeled, so it is illuminating to examine the history and some of the actual scientific studies that have been conducted on some of these chemicals.

In general, drugs such as methamphetamine, heroin and cocaine are addictive, are toxic to the point of easily killing you if overdosed, and have a tendency to ruin people's lives. The DEA classifies marijuana and psychedelics in the same category as these other drugs, despite the fact that nobody has ever died of a marijuana overdose. The faulty reasoning runs like this: Methamphetamine and heroin are addictive, toxic, and destroy peoples' lives and should be illegal. Methamphetamine and heroin are drugs. Marijuana, psilocybin mushrooms and ayahuasca are also drugs. Therefore marijuana, mushrooms and ayahuasca should also be illegal. A brief review of the actual facts about these substances will clearly point out how illogical this is.

Let's start with marijuana, more appropriately known as cannabis. The common name for cannabis is hemp, an extremely useful agricultural crop the fibers and oils from which can be used for textiles, foods, papers, health care products, detergents, plastics and building materials. Some varieties have additionally been bred to have higher concentrations of chemicals such as THC (Tetrahydrocannabinoids), the intoxicating ingredients that make you high, and other chemicals that have medicinal value. Hemp is so useful in so many different industries that it was perceived as a threat to owners of some other industries.

In the early 1930's, Henry Ford made a car with a plastic body which was composed of 70% hemp and straw fibers and 30% hemp resin binder that had 10 times the impact strength of its steel counterparts. There is an old film showing Henry Ford himself hitting the body of this car with a sledge hammer and not denting or even scratching it, so resilient was the hemp plastic used in its construction. Because there was so much less steel used in its construction, the car weighed 1000 lbs less than it would have had it been made from conventional materials. The seats were woven from hemp cloth. The car even ran on ethanol made from hemp oil.

This was clearly a better way to go - we could grow the materials to make our cars as well as the fuel to run them with a renewable resource rather than extracting iron and oil out of the earth, resources that existed in a finite supply. But powerful men who became powerful by owning oil fields and steel and paper mills were not about to have the source of their power undercut by Henry Ford's ingenuity; hemp had to be brought down if they were to maintain their exorbitant wealth.

Probably the biggest player in making cannabis illegal was William Randolph Hearst, the newspaper tycoon. In the mid-1930's, new innovations in agricultural technology allowed for the invention of a mechanical method of processing hemp. With this breakthrough, the Industrial Hemp Industry was poised to replace wood as an inexpensive raw material for the production of paper.

Hearst had invested in millions of acres of timberland to supply wood pulp, as well as in wood pulp papermaking equipment, for his paper and media industries. If hemp were to succeed, Hearst would lose a tremendous amount of money. Hearst started a smear campaign against hemp, utilizing his huge chain of newspapers to print stories about the evils of hemp. Not only did this help to influence public opinion, it also turned out that telling lurid lies about the "devil marijuana weed" causing acts of violence sold newspapers and helped make Hearst even richer.

Some examples of stories printed in Hearst's papers:

"Marihuana makes fiends of boys in thirty days — Hashish goads users to bloodlust."

"By the tons it is coming into this country — the deadly, dreadful poison that racks and tears not only the body, but the very heart and soul of every human being who once becomes a slave to it in any of its cruel and devastating forms.... Marihuana is a short cut to the insane asylum. Smoke marihuana cigarettes for a month and what was once your brain will be nothing but a storehouse of horrid specters. Hasheesh makes a murderer who kills for the love of killing out of the mildest mannered man who ever laughed at the idea that any habit could ever get him...."

"Users of marijuana become STIMULATED as they inhale the drug and are LIKELY TO DO ANYTHING. Most crimes of violence in this section, especially in country districts are laid to users of that drug."

"Was it marijuana, the new Mexican drug, that nerved the murderous arm of Clara Phillips when she hammered out her victim's life in Los Angeles?... THREE-FOURTHS OF THE CRIMES of violence in this country today are committed by DOPE SLAVES — that is a matter of cold record."

Hearst had plenty of support from other industrialists who also stood to benefit from making cannabis illegal. Andrew Mellon, founder of Gulf Oil Corporation, certainly didn't want to see hemp's usefulness as an alternative raw material for fuel and plastics compete with his oil profits. Mellon served as Secretary of the Treasury, and used his influence to create the Federal Bureau of Narcotics. He then appointed his own future nephew-in-law, Harry Anslinger, as director. Anslinger made use of the fabricated sensational articles published by Hearst, to push the Marijuana Tax Act of 1937 through Congress. This act successfully destroyed the rebirth of the cannabis hemp industry.

A third major player was the du Pont Family, who had tremendous influence in both the government and private sector. The du Pont Chemical Corporation owned the patents on synthetic petrochemicals and industrial processes used for making wood pulp paper using a new sulfate/sulfite process, gasoline additives, synthetic fibers such as their newly introduced "miracle" fiber nylon, and in 1937 patented the process for making plastics from oil and coal. Du Pont stood to make billions of dollars from these patents if hemp was suppressed.

The very word marijuana was coined at that time because it sounded foreign and would confuse people who normally would have supported hemp into thinking they were talking about another plant entirely. This is why I prefer to use the word cannabis, as "marijuana" was created as part of the lie used to make hemp illegal.

Eventually the bill came to the House of Representatives for a vote. Earlier that day, William C. Woodward, representing the American Medical

Association, testified that the AMA was strongly opposed to this legislation, that there was no medical reason to make cannabis illegal, and pointed out many inconsistencies and fabrication of "evidence" being used to support the bill. Unfortunately, most members of the house were not present for his testimony. And when it came time to vote, the entire conversation went as follows:

Member from upstate New York: *"Mr. Speaker, what is this bill about?"*

Speaker Rayburn: *"I don't know. It has something to do with a thing called marihuana. I think it's a narcotic of some kind."*

"Mr. Speaker, does the American Medical Association support this bill?"

Member on the committee jumps up and says: *"Their Doctor Wentworth came down here. They support this bill 100 percent."*

And so thanks to that lie, on that day in August, 1937, marijuana became illegal at the federal level.

So clearly it was not concern over cannabis's harmful effects on the brain or body that got it made illegal. Nor have those negative effects been found to be there by good fortune since the bill was passed. One of the few studies that claim adverse effects from cannabis, and one that the federal government sites when justifying the continued ban, was done by Dr. Heath in 1974.

Dr. Heath carried out experiments on Rhesus monkeys by tying them down and forcing them to inhale the equivalent of 63 joints through a gas mask in five minutes. After this he killed the monkeys and examined their brains, comparing the count of dead cells to a control group. Not too surprisingly, the marijuana group had a much higher count of dead brain cells, but it wasn't from the cannabis; rather, it was due to extreme carbon monoxide poisoning from the huge amount of smoke inhaled.

This study is generally regarded to be worthless as the monkeys were actually suffocated to death by carbon monoxide poisoning and oxygen deprivation, yet it is still frequently cited as proof that cannabis is harmful; in 1974 California Governor Ronald Reagan referred to this study when he said in an L.A. Times interview "The most reliable scientific sources say permanent brain damage is one of the inevitable results of the use of marijuana".

The other study that is frequently cited as proof of cannabis's toxicity was done by Dr. Gabriel Nahas of Columbia University in 1972. Nahas claimed his studies showed that marijuana caused chromosome and testosterone damage as well as ill effects on the immune system. However, no anti-marijuana studies of his have ever been replicated in many other research attempts. The National Institutes of Health has forbidden him from further funding because of his shoddy research, and Columbia University specifically disassociated itself from his research in 1975.

So how toxic is cannabis, then? There has never been a proven documented cannabis-induced fatality, not a single record of such in any of the extensive medical literature. More accurate research than Heath's or Nahas' has shown that is would take 20,000 to 40,000 times as much marijuana as is contained in one marijuana cigarette to reach a lethal dose. To reach this dose the smoker would have to consume almost 1,500 pounds of marijuana within 15 minutes. Clearly this is never going to happen.

Cannabis is actually classified under a broader class of drugs known as psychedelics, although the consciousness-altering effects are much less pronounced than what is commonly seen with other drugs in this class, such as LSD, psilocybin (found in "magic mushrooms"), MDMA, DMT (see chapter 24) and Salvia divinorum. Though these are the most commonly known psychedelics, there are actually quite a few more examples, with more being synthesized and tested all the time.

Psychedelics as a class are generally quite different from the more dangerous and addictive drugs found in the classifications of stimulants and opioids. For most psychedelic drugs, including the most commonly used ones such as magic mushrooms and LSD, there has never been a recorded lethal overdose. Psychedelics used in research in the 1950s and 60s consistently showed extremely low incidences of either acute or chronic problems except in some cases where there was a pre-existing severe psychopathology.

Later studies, studies that were funded by the government, have shown harmful effects on the brain, but follow-up studies by independent scientists have consistently been unable to replicate the results and in fact have generally shown that psychedelics generally have minimal deleterious effects and often have surprisingly beneficial effects.

Take for example 3,4-methylenedioxymeth-amphetamine, or MDMA, commonly called "ecstasy". When it was first synthesized, it was found to have interesting effects on the serotonin receptors in the brain, effects that made the owner of that brain feel connected and in love with everyone and everything around them. It did this by temporarily lowering the psychological walls people put between themselves and others. But it also lowered the walls between different parts of the psyche, and this allowed more communication and self-acceptance between the conscious and the subconscious and between the different parts of the subconscious.

This was extremely valuable for therapy, a miracle antidote for emotionally distraught and traumatized people, and there were some promising results when used with schizophrenia, whose sufferers have particularly high walls between different parts of their psyches.

But MDMA also had the effect of making the user feel really good. After all, it feels nice to be in love with everyone around you. And so it rapidly became popular as a recreational drug, especially at raves.

Somebody at the DEA wanted it stopped, but to do so they needed to show MDMA was harmful. A study done in 1985 by George Ricaurte and Charles Schuster at the University of Chicago seemed to fit the bill. In this study, MDA (a related but different chemical with somewhat similar mental effects) was given to rats at 10 times the usual dose (per pound of body weight), and this dose was repeated every four hours for two days, after which the (presumably extremely happy) rats were sacrificed and had their brains examined under a microscope.

This examination did reveal some structural changes in the terminals where serotonin interfaces with brain cells, a minor amount of brain damage that is actually less than what has been seen with some other perfectly legal pharmaceuticals given at less extreme doses, but nevertheless was the basis for claiming the drug was dangerous which resulted in making it illegal.

Later studies, funded by the government, showed even more dramatic harmful effects on the brain, claiming that 50% to 85% of the brain's serotonin was irreversibly destroyed by MDMA use (McCann UD, Szabo Z, Scheffel U, Dannals RF, Ricaurte GA. Positron emission tomographic evidence of toxic effect of MDMA ("ecstasy") on brain serotonin neurons in human beings. Lancet 1998;352:1433–1437), and that Parkinson's disease could be induced by even one usage of the psychedelic.

These studies where later shown to be based on faulty data. The Parkinson's disease claim was from a study using monkeys who were in fact given methamphetamine, not MDMA as claimed. And in 2002 the prestigious British journal New Scientist challenged the United States government's position on MDMA. The journal had leading independent scientists look at the evidence and could not conclude that MDMA was incontrovertibly dangerous; the best they could come up with was that "the jury is still out".

Then a German study published in 2003 showed only a mild 4% to 5% Serotonin loss in the brains of ecstasy users, and a return to normal levels after 2 or 3 months of abstaining from ecstasy, a far cry from the previously claimed permanent loss of up to 85%. Only a handful of deaths have been attributed to ecstasy, and most of those were in fact due to contamination from other substances added to lower the cost of the street drug or to interactions from concurrent multiple drug use. Only a couple of cases can be attributed solely to MDMA, out of hundreds of millions of users. By this measure MDMA is in fact safer than aspirin, a drug readily available over the counter.

Let's look at one more example. Hallucinogenic mushrooms, often referred to as "magic mushrooms", contain a chemical called psilocybin which causes the psychedelic experience from consuming these mushrooms. There are numerous studies that show positive long term benefits from either consuming the hallucinogenic mushrooms themselves or from ingesting synthesized psilocybin.

One such study was published in the journal *Psychopharmacology* (Psilocybin can occasion mystical-type experiences having substantial and sustained personal meaning and spiritual significance. Psychopharmacology (2006) 187:268–283). In their study, scientists from Johns Hopkins School of Medicine induced transcendental experiences in volunteers utilizing psilocybin, which resulted in long-lasting psychological growth and helped people find peace in their lives, without any negative effects.

The study involved 18 healthy adults, average age 46, who participated in five eight-hour sessions with either varying doses of psilocybin or a placebo. Fourteen months after participating in the study, 94% of those who received the drug said the experiment was one of the top five most meaningful experiences of their lives; 39% said it was the single most meaningful experience.

It is interesting to note that it was not just the participants themselves who saw the benefit from participating in the study; their family members, friends and colleagues also reported that after utilizing psilocybin the participants were calmer, happier and kinder. Another study published in Archives of General Psychiatry in 2011 found that people with anxiety who were given a single psilocybin treatment had decreased depression scores six months later (Pilot study of psilocybin treatment for anxiety in patients with advanced-stage cancer. Arch Gen Paychiatry. 2011 Jan; 68(1):71-8).

And as to safety, this is again another drug with no confirmed deaths. The LD50 (the dose at which you would have a 50% chance of dying) in rats is 280 mg/kg, administered through an injection. An average size human would have to eat about four pounds of dried mushrooms to get this dose. A typical dose of mushrooms is about a sixteenth of an ounce, which makes the toxic dose about 1000 times the therapeutic dose. Most legal pharmaceuticals have nowhere near this safety margin.

I have a close personal friend who once ate two pounds of mushrooms in one sitting. Now I am not in any way recommending this. This individual is a bit, well, extreme, and his experience after consuming this huge amount of mushrooms was equally extreme. But the point is that, after about 3 days, he returned to normal, perfectly healthy. And he says that the experience changed his life in nothing but positive ways.

And that's the remarkable thing about psychedelics. Users consistently say that using psychedelics changed their lives in positive ways. You just don't hear that from heroine users, or from methamphetamine users, or from cocaine users.

Oh, they might say that using cocaine is fun, or feels good, but they never say it changed their lives in positive ways. And this is backed up in another study, this time by researchers at the Norwegian University of Science and Technology. Their study, following more than 20,000 psychedelic users, found that usage of psychedelics was not linked with mental health problems, and in fact in some cases actually seemed to promote better mental health (LSD and other psychedelics not linked with mental health problems. Plos One, August 19, 2013).

The researchers found that use of psilocybin, mescaline and LSD were associated with lower rates of serious psychological distress, and that "many people report deeply meaningful experiences and lasting beneficial effects from using psychedelics." The author concludes: "Over the past 50 years, tens of millions of people have used psychedelics and there just is not much evidence of long-term problems."

So, now that we have gotten past the "all drugs are bad" argument, let's explore how chemicals can help explore consciousness. The chemicals I'm referring to, of course, are psychedelics. Altering your consciousness is a great way to become aware of your consciousness. Just as a fish is unaware of the water it resides in, an unaltered consciousness is difficult to "see" without occasionally stepping outside of it and observing it from an altered state. People who enjoy exploring consciousness from altered perspectives often refer to themselves as "psychonauts".

A change in perspective, even a temporary one, can make a big difference in how we see things. A single perspective is like looking with only one eye. A second, new, perspective, from a second eye, can add a whole new dimension to our vision, especially when we hold both perspectives at the same time. This works even when the two perspectives are quite similar, as is the case with our eyes, which are less than two inches apart. Just that slight shift in perspective is enough to give us three dimensional vision.

The same is true with a shift of our psychological perspective, whether it is initiated by psychedelics or some other means. And it is just as difficult to explain what that's like to someone who has never shifted their perspective chemically as is would be to try to explain three dimensional vision to someone born with only one eye.

I have already mentioned some of the insights I have had using ayahuasca, whose active ingredient is Dimethyltryptamine, or DMT (see chapter 24). I have also found that combining some of these chemicals with other practices, such as meditation (see chapter 24) or ecstatic dance (see chapter 23) can greatly deepen the experience. This is what raves are all about - combining dance with chemical modulation.

Though not technically an ecstatic dance as far as the rhythms go, the dancing at raves still tends to be guided by what is deep within and so can be a form of dynamic meditation. The chemical enhancement used is typically ecstasy, and rave music is specifically designed to mesh with this particular psychedelic. Ecstasy causes a particular frequency resonance in the body of 120 bpm, and as the music pounds at that frequency, it resonates with and deepens the psychedelic experience, while at the same time the psychedelic experience deepens the music experience.

This is also true of ayahuasca ceremonies - the music and chanting done during the ceremonies are chosen to resonate with and deepen the ayahuasca experience. I have had profound experiences and deep insights at raves. Some of the insights I can try to relay, but the experience of the different perspective is much more difficult to translate.

While dancing, I will often go deeply into the music, and for several moments will lose my sense of self, lose awareness of my body, my thought process, or any sense of "I", and essentially become the music. I also lose my sense of time, so the moments I am in this state feel simultaneously like no time at all and infinitely long (see chapter 18). I come away from it with vague memories of pulses of light in strange patterns, but not really a visual experience so much as some different experience that my brain tries to interpret visually.

It is almost as though my consciousness gets lifted out of my brain and into a different dimension, a dimension with sensations that are not the usual sight/sound/smell/taste/touch but something else entirely. Afterward I try to fit the experience into the three-dimensional world with which I'm familiar but it's like trying to describe the concept of "color" to someone who has been blind all their life. It feels like a deep meditative state, without all the bother of meditating. It also feels very, very important, and I want to go back there again and again until I can understand it.

Other times the experience I bring back from these other dimensions is more concrete and understandable, though I don't always remember what they were after the chemicals fade. For that reason many years ago I started to write down my insights, the ones I could understand and remember, as soon as I was able to. The insights seemed too important to let fad away, and I found I had a pretty good knack for translating the gestalt of the insight and experience into a linear flow of English. Much of what I came to understand and write down ended up fitting perfectly into this very book you are now reading, some of the chapters being almost exactly what I had written down years ago and needing almost no editing at all.

I remember at one rave I attended I was having a series of insights, one after another. Each one was a new perspective on life that seemed so important that it appeared to be obvious that having such an insight is the whole reason I was at the party in the first place, my reason to live, the Ultimate Answer to Life, the Universe, and Everything.

Each Insight came to me as one gestalt, complete in one moment. I would start to put words to it in order to nail it down in my brain so I could remember it, but before getting very far I was on to the next insight, and the first insight got lost. At one point during the rave I had an insight that I felt I really wanted to take back with me. I even was able to summarize it into a couple of sentences. I pulled myself off of the dance floor, pulled out my cell phone, and texted it to myself so I would have it for later.

What I texted was "I'm the central character in my story; damn right I'm going to write a great part for it." I remember feeling as though I had complete control over how my life played out, and as long as I maintained a state of mindfulness I could insure that the story of my life was exciting and fun and full of joy and love and wonderful experiences and would have a happy ending.

Several times during the night I would start to feel tired and it became hard to move to keep dancing. Then I would say to myself: "Wait, I don't want to be the guy in the story who gets tired and stops dancing at 4:00 am, I want to be the guy who, in his 50s, has the energy to keep dancing without feeling tired all night long". And then I would become that guy, step into that role, and the tiredness would melt away.

This ability to change the story line turns out to be something that is not just limited to altered conscious states, but can be done in our "normal" consciousness as well. It is as though we wake up to the fact that we are dreaming, and can decide to take control of the dream and manipulate it to our liking, even though it is "real".

And yet . . . as we row, row, row our boat, gently down the stream, we, with the help of altered consciousness (either chemically or otherwise), may come to realize that life is indeed "but a dream". That there is a deeper, more "real" reality that underlies what we think of as reality. And that we can awaken from this dream that we call reality and bring our consciousness back into resonance with that other deeper reality.

Part 3 - Waking From the Dream

Chapter 28 - Freedom

What limits your freedom? Prison bars? An oppressive government? A domineering spouse? Social convention? Fear? Emotional wounds that trigger irrational reactions? Those pesky laws of physics? The weak enslave themselves, sure, but that only seems to apply to those lower down on the freedom ladder. The thrill of breaking the chains is almost worth having the chains in the first place. Viva la revolución.

Ultimately, we have no freedom if we have no free will, no matter the lack of prison bars, etc. We may feel as though we have free will, but experiments with brain scans suggest that, in certain situations at least, free will may be an illusion.

Ben Libet's work with computer and EEG scans of the brain in the 1980's showed that the subconscious mind knows how we will act before our conscious mind makes a decision to act. (Libet, Benjamin et al (1983). "Time of Conscious Intention to Act in Relation to Onset of Cerebral Activity (Readiness-Potential) - The Unconscious Initiation of a Freely Voluntary Act". *Brain* **106**: 623–642. doi:10.1093/brain/106.3.623.PMID 6640273, and Libet, Benjamin (1985). "Unconscious Cerebral Initiative and the Role of Conscious Will in Voluntary Action". *The Behavioral and Brain Sciences* **8**: 529–

566.doi:10.1017/s0140525x00044903.) Later work utilizing fMRI not only confirmed this, but also showed that our actions could be predicted a full seven seconds prior to consciously making a decision (see chapter 24). If our decisions can be predicted several seconds before we consciously will to act, can our actions really said to be the result of free will?

If we do have free will, these experiments would indicate that it resides in our subconscious, and our conscious mind is merely along for the ride (see chapter 24). But free agency must be conscious for us to feel we have free will; if one is always acting out of their subconscious, can they really be said to be free?

So do you have free will? That depends on where "you" are. If your sense of self resides in the ceaseless chatter of the ego, then, no, I don't believe you do, as much as the ego would like to believe otherwise. Neither do you have free will if your sense of self resides in your physical body, your memories, your thoughts, your perceptions or your expectations.

To be free, you must bring "you" deeper, until you are resting in simple awareness. Here, you bring your consciousness to the subconscious, where our free will actually resides. It is only from here that "you" can access your free will (see also chapter 25).

Chapter 29 - Attitude

In my work as a veterinarian, I have often seen dogs who arrive at my clinic all happy and excited, expecting that this will be another fun outing. And sure enough, there are all these new people who are happy to see him, and are doting on him and giving him treats. There might be a moment or two where some weird thing happens, something gets briefly shoved up his butt or there might be a brief moment of discomfort while some blood is drawn, but it isn't that bad and afterwards everybody is so proud of him and are giving more treats and he has a great time lapping it all up.

The next dog to come in, though, might have an entirely different experience. He's suspicious about where his guardian is taking him. Maybe he's sensing his guardian's tension, who is remembering the last disastrous visit to the vet. His fears are soon confirmed as strange people surround him and violate him by sticking some unknown strange object up his anus – what's wrong with these people?!?

Soon the ringleader enters and rudely looks at every part of his body, poking at him with his fingers. These strange people try to bribe him with enticing bits of food, but the dog suspects that it is a trap or that they contain poison, and cleverly refuses. But his refusal seems to prompt their anger, for the next thing that happens is harrowing: the people surround and hold the poor dog firmly while the ringleader takes his front leg and does something painful; it feels like a small bite although the ringleader's head didn't go near the leg.

In any event, after this new round of torture is completed, these horrible people try once again to offer him the suspicious food. Afraid of more torture, the dog reluctantly takes it in his mouth, but then can't bring himself to swallow the poison and risks more torture by dropping it on the floor. The ringleader seems disappointed, then picks up the food and drops it in the garbage! Ah hah! Proof that it was poisoned; otherwise the ringleader would have surely eaten it himself! Finally he is able to escape this horrifying place, secure in the knowledge that his suspicions were right all along.

The interesting thing about these two very different experiences is that the environments were the same, the people were the same, the actual level of danger was the same and everything that was done to the first dog was done to the second. The only difference is in the two dogs' attitudes. Their expectations and perceptions were the only thing that made one experience extremely enjoyable and the other miserable.

We have the ability to choose our attitude, which in turn determines the kind of experiences we have. Why not choose an attitude that makes life more enjoyable? Ah, you say, but what if the world really is a dangerous place? What if the treat really had been poisoned? Wouldn't the second dog's behavior been more appropriate for that situation? Not necessarily; he still would have had a more miserable experience, for one thing.

Paranoia is still paranoia, even if they really are out to get you. But beyond that, according to Biocentrism and proven by quantum mechanics, there really is no objectifiable "out there", no reality until we observe it. We create reality from our Shadow, give it form with our filters and color it with our expectations. The world is really a dangerous place only if we believe it is a dangerous place.

Yes, some "bad" things might happen from time to time, but these things are only "bad" because we put that judgment upon them. From another perspective they may not look bad at all. We create our universe from our Shadow; that which we do not deal with in our Shadow manifests in the world around us to deal with there (where it is, unfortunately, often more difficult to deal with) (see chapters 15 and 21).

So, "bad" things are in actuality opportunities for healing wounded parts of our Shadow. This is what

Gandhi referred to when he said to be the change you want to see in the world. Transformation occurs when our perspective shifts.

Of course, it's not just dogs who create their reality with their attitude and expectations. My wife and I put on two different ecstatic dances. There is only one main difference between the dances - one is specifically gender-balanced and the other is not. Our original non-gender-balanced dance typically has attracted twice as many men as women. We have found that sometimes some new women will attend, see the preponderance of men, feel overwhelmed, and leave, thus adding to the imbalance.

The point of the dance was not to match up men with women, so there was not really a problem with it being imbalanced. But still, there is a different energy in a room full of mostly men than there is in a room full of mostly women or a room with a balance of both. And we wanted to create a space where the women who felt overwhelmed and were not attending our regular dance could feel safe to attend. So we created a second dance that people had to sign up for, and only let in enough men to balance the women who signed up. Since this is more work on our parts, we charge more for this dance, but otherwise it is pretty much the exact same dance.

What we have found is that for our gender-balanced dance very often we end up having no men on the waiting list. By creating the intention of a gender-balanced dance, we attracted enough women automatically to balance the men. So what this means is that when the women, as a group, were afraid that there would be too many men, they manifested that exact situation from their fear. But when they could let go of fear by believing that somebody else would take care of that situation for them, they ended up manifesting a balanced situation for themselves.

The two examples above are situations where it is easy to see how reality can be manifested, but the principle is the same for all aspects of our lives. We manifest everything that happens to us. Sometimes we manifest from our fears and sometimes we manifest from our hopes. But ultimately it is all us, consciously or unconsciously, manifesting our situations and authoring the story of our lives. Doing it consciously works better.

Chapter 30 – How to Change Reality

We have been taught to believe that there is a reality out there, independent of us. It existed before we were born and will go on existing after we die, and our role in shaping it is relatively minor. Evidence is accumulating that this is not the case. Experiments in quantum physics are showing us that the nature of reality is highly dependent on who is observing it. One of the best known of these experiments is known as the two slit experiment.

If one were to shoot a shotgun at a wall with a single slit in it with another wall beyond the slit, one would find a pattern of hits on the far wall that form a single straight line. If there were two slits, one would find two straight lines. If you fire something considerably smaller than birdshot at the slits, such as electrons, you find something surprising.

When the electrons go through the slits, they end up forming not two straight lines but an interference pattern on the far wall. The reason for this is that the electrons, though they act like little balls of something making one dot when they hit the far wall, actually travel to that wall as a wave. The waves interfere with each other, in some places augmenting, in other places canceling each other out, to form the interference pattern. In the world of the tiny, things can act as both a wave and a particle at the same time.

It really becomes interesting when the electrons are fired at the slits one at a time. If the electrons are coming through the slits one at a time, they couldn't possibly be interfered with by another electron. However, when this is done the same interference pattern emerges. The only explanation for this is that the electron actually travels through both slits at the same time, interferes with itself after it passes through, and then finally collapses into a particle at one spot on the far wall in a location consistent with the interference pattern.

Now here's where things really get weird. If the experimenter puts a detector at the slits in order to determine which slit the electron passed through before it hits its spot on the far wall, the interference pattern suddenly disappears and is replaced by two straight lines like one saw with the birdshot. Remember, this detector in no way interacts with the electrons; it simply records them as they pass by. Somehow the electron "knows" whether or not it is being observed, and changes its behavior accordingly.

What this experiment shows us is that it is the act of observing that collapses the probability wave, which is the summation of all the possible realities, into the one reality that is observed. And it is our perspective, our experience and our filters that determine what it is that we are able to observe. Change the filters, and we change the reality.

Our conscious minds are only able to process about 200 bits of information at a time, out of the 11 million bits of information it receives every second. This is like taking a trip around the entire planet Earth, but only being aware of 5 blocks of our journey and extrapolating what the rest of the planet must look like from the information in that tiny slice. Think of how different reality could potentially look like if we just let in a different slice. Each of us creates our own universe with our consciousness as a black hole in the center of it, simply by the act of observing reality from our unique perspective.

All physical laws, every object we encounter, everything that makes up our version of reality, can be thought of as a web, one which we wove ourselves and which is everything to us. Other people live in their own webs. When we communicate with each other, we exchange information about what our webs look like, and make the mistake of assuming we're talking about the same web.

If there is a difference between our webs, we conclude that the other person is mistaken, perhaps even to the point of insanity. And sometimes we alter our web to fit what others are telling us about their web, especially if 100 other monkeys say the same thing.

When scientists first theorized that subatomic particles called neutrinos should exist, they devised experiments intended to detect them and measure their attributes. This was during the time of the cold war, and both American and Soviet scientists conducted experiments independently of each other. Both sets of scientists obtained good consistent data about neutrinos, but when the two groups started finally talking to each other, they found that their results differed from each other.

What is interesting is that after the two groups communicated, repeated experiments started yielding data that was consistent between them. Physical laws concerning neutrinos changed to fit the observer's expectations. Their webs shifted to appear to be the same to both groups.

Web-altering tends to be subconscious and automatic, but it can be done consciously and with intention. There are three levels of reality-shifting, and we tend to master them one level at a time. Level I involves minor shifts that could be easily explained away by chance; it is only the consistency of the occurrences that help us know that it's working. Examples include manifesting parking spaces or changing the weather.

Level II involves more dramatic shifts that make even skeptics say "hmmmm" – creating highly unlikely shifts that still fall within the realm of the possible. Examples include winning the lottery or manifesting sitting down on the airplane next to the one person on the planet that you needed to talk to.

Level III involves performing miracles – shifts from our presently understood reality so dramatic as to be unable to be explained by chance at any odds. Examples include instantly healing broken bones and levitation.

One good way to start reality shifting is to connect deeply with someone else, especially someone who views the world from a very different perspective from you. Find ways in which their view of reality differs from yours. Look at those differences without judgment as to who is "right" and who is "wrong". Decide which version you like better. Adopt the preferable version.

Another good way to shift Reality is to change your attitude (see chapter 29). Anything you put energy into will tend to grow, and this includes the energy from our attention. If we put our attention on what we're grateful for in this life and stop giving our attention to what no longer serves us, we can relatively easily tip the balance in our favor and manifest more things in our lives to be grateful for.

Chapter 31 - Non-Newtonian Fluids as a Model of the Quantum Flux and the Creation of Reality Via Observation

A non-Newtonian fluid is a fluid whose viscosity depends on the force that is applied to it. When corn starch is suspended in water, it forms such a fluid. When poured or stirred slowly, it flows like water, but with any kind of a kinetic impact, it instantly acts solid. This allows a person to run across the top of a pool of corn starch, but if they stop, they will suddenly sink into it (for good examples, see www.youtube.com/watch?v=amfjWWMg9c0 and www.youtube.com/watch?v=f2XQ97XHjVw).

You can also roll a bowling ball across the surface of the corn starch, and as long as it keeps rolling, the ball will provide the kinetic impact to keep the fluid acting as a solid. Once it stops rolling, however, the bowling ball will sink into the liquid (see www.youtube.com/watch?v=8SEB0Nhx5TU).

It's even more interesting to watch the corn starch suspension react to vibrations, such as from a speaker. Each pulse from the speaker will momentarily freeze the solution into a solid, and unusual and complex shapes will appear out of the soup that grow and evolve as the music continues to pulse (www.youtube.com/watch?v=nq3ZjY0Uf-g

and www.youtube.com/watch?v=WaYvYysQvBU).

The quantum flux collapses into reality in much the same way, with the act of observation acting as the kinetic impact on the non-Newtonian fluid. We tend to think of time as a strict linear progression from cause to effect, and space as being made up of distinct locations that either do or do not contain specific particles or objects. But from a non-linear, non-subjective perspective, space and time are more like a big ball of indeterminate constantly shifting stuff.

The true nature of reality is a probability wave that contains within it every possible configuration of space and time, all existing without any true form in a soup of possibility. At the moment this quantum flux is observed, however, the probability wave instantly collapses into what we think of as the true reality. The act of observation acts as the kinetic impact on a non-Newtonian fluid that instantly crystallizes the quantum flux into a reality pattern that is both self-consistent and dependent on the perspective of the one doing the observing.

Of course, the reality that we observe is a much more complex wave pattern than what we see in corn starch, but even a simple sine wave can create remarkably complex forms in the corn starch. And when we stop observing the quantum flux, it all flows back into the indeterminate stuff, ready to re-solidify again with the next observation, the specific wave pattern being dependent upon our perspective and expectations, which in turn is generally dependent upon the specific wave pattern that coalesced from the impact of our previous act of observation.

There are an infinite number of possible wave forms, as well as an infinite number that are not self-consistent and therefore not possible. It is the mind that determines whether a wave form is self-consistent and therefore possible to observe. And it is our experiences and expectations that determine which of the possible wave forms is most likely to manifest, just as it is the form of the glob of corn starch that helps determine the next shape of the glob of corn starch when the next pulse from the speaker hits. Changing our expectations can influence which wave form manifests, within the confines of what the mind determines to be possible.

Chapter 32 - The Shape of Time

All of our possible futures lay in front of us, some of them directly ahead and easy to reach, others off to the side and more difficult to reach. As time marches ahead, more and more of our potential futures drop over the event horizon and become impossible, until finally when the present moment is reached only one possible future remains and becomes NOW. See figure 1.

Figure 1

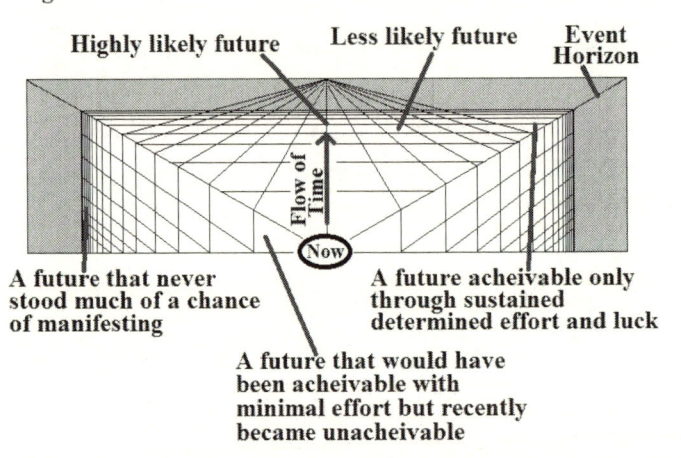

Highly likely future — Less likely future — Event Horizon

Flow of Time

Now

A future that never stood much of a chance of manifesting

A future acheivable only through sustained determined effort and luck

A future that would have been acheivable with minimal effort but recently became unacheivable

The more possible pathways to a possible future, the more likely it will be ahead of us on the plane of possibilities and the more likely it might end up as a NOW. Similarly, the possible futures with fewer possible pathways yield decreasing probabilities and lie nearer the event horizon (see figure 2).

Figure 2

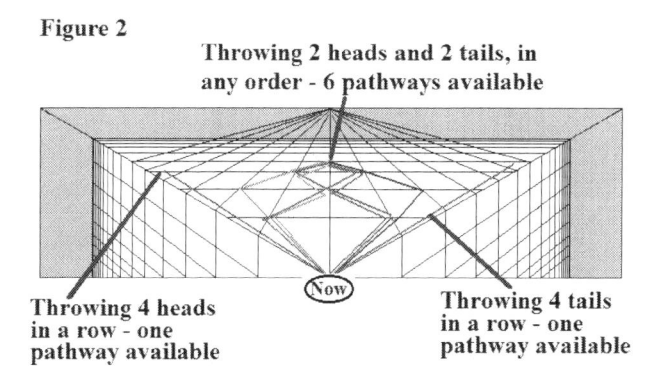

Throwing 2 heads and 2 tails, in any order - 6 pathways available

Throwing 4 heads in a row - one pathway available

Throwing 4 tails in a row - one pathway available

Now

Most people assume that once a possible future passes through NOW, it becomes fixed as our actual past for all time, but I do not believe this is so. There are many different possible pasts, any one of which could potentially have led us to the NOW we find ourselves in, and the further back in time you look, the more possible pasts there are (see figure 3). This ends up giving Time sort of an hour-glass shape, which is rather appropriate.

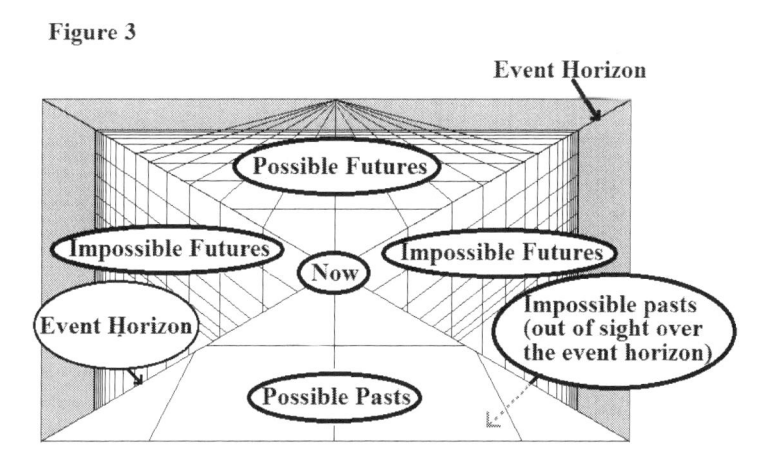

Figure 3

Event Horizon

Possible Futures

Impossible Futures

Impossible Futures

Now

Event Horizon

Impossible pasts (out of sight over the event horizon)

Possible Pasts

For example, let's say you are driving down a road, and you are stuck behind a slow car. You decide to pass, and shortly after you do, the car turns off the road and then you end up stopped at a traffic light. At this point you have ended up exactly where you would have been had you not passed, with the exception of your memory of the event. As soon as you forget whether you passed or not, there becomes no difference in the universe wherein you decided to pass and the one wherein you did not, and both pasts are equally likely to have led to the present NOW.

Both possible pasts did in fact happen, the universe split into two, one in which you passed and one in which you did not, and then those two universes merged back into one when you forgot about it (see figure 4). During the phase where the only difference exists in our memory, we can change the past by remembering it differently, and thus shifting onto the alternate past universe.

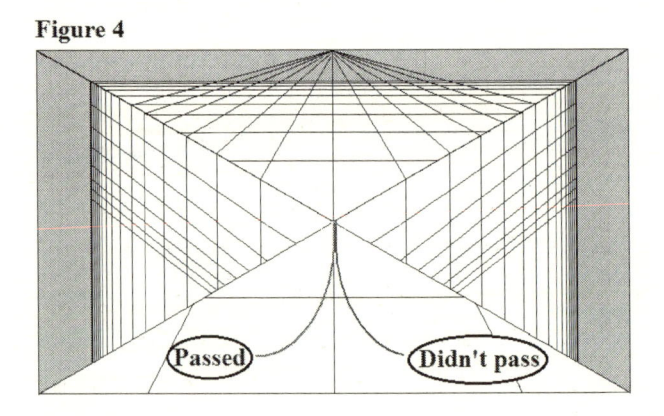

Figure 4

The exception to all this is when there was a car coming the other way when you decided to pass, and you ended up in an accident. Now the pass/don't pass decision point becomes a Fixed Point in Time, and remains fixed until such point as it again makes no difference.

This could be a matter of years until you have the ding knocked out and eventually forget all about it. Or it could take generations, if you ended up dying in the accident while your alternate self in the didn't-pass universe has one or more children, the universes finally merging when your entire line dies out and becomes forgotten. Or it could take thousands of years if one of your progeny ends up making a significant contribution to history. Eventually, every possible past will end up becoming as significant as any other when our sun expands into a red giant and engulfs the Earth, unless we have colonized the stars by then.

Every possible future lay ahead of the infant universe at the moment of the Big Bang, and every possible past will lay behind and lead up to the Big Crunch at the end of the universe. At the end of the universe, every possible universe merges into one. Everything between the Big Bang and the Big Crunch exists as a quantum flux of possibilities, one big multiverse containing every possible chain of cause and effect.

Our consciousnesses float through this quantum fog, collapsing it into local pockets of "reality" with our awareness, but those collapsed pockets of reality is not Time's true form. To quote Dr. Who: "people assume that time is a strict progression of cause to effect, but actually from a non-linear, non-subjective viewpoint, it's more like a big ball of wibbly wobbly timey wimey stuff."

By focusing and putting energy into preferable possible futures, we increase their likelihood of eventually manifesting as a NOW, especially if we leave the specific pathway up to our higher selves, whose vantage point affords a clearer view of the optimum pathway. In the same way, focusing on preferable pasts, remembering things the way we wish they had happened, puts energy into and grows those pasts we prefer. It's important to be optimistic about both our futures and our pasts.

Chapter 33 - The Causal Nexus

Whenever you observe anyone or anything, you collapse the waveform of all the possible ways that person or thing can be into one solid object. This may seem as though the observer has a special place in the universe, the only one with permanent existence, with everybody else flitting in and out of existence as they are observed or not observed, but bear with me and we will see that this is not so.

Let's say we observe someone, and in that moment they are in a particular place, looking and acting a particular way. When we stop observing them, we no longer know how they are acting, which way they are moving, etc. In fact, from our perspective at least, when we stop observing them, they move in all directions (or at least all possible directions - left or right, say, but never straight up – see chapter 34) and act in all possible ways (angry or happy, say, but never in ways inconsistent with their personality).

Their existence (again, from our perspective, not theirs) becomes fuzzy, shifting from a point of certainty to an expanding ball of possibility. And if we then observe them again, we again collapse that ball into a point. Repeating this process produces an existence that looks like pearls on a string, with the string portions, or the nodes between the pearls, representing their collapsed state that is defined by your observation, the smaller pearls representing those moments when you look away for a short period of time, and the larger pearls representing those times when you look away for longer periods of time.

As someone comes repeatedly in and out of your life, you repeatedly define their existence - not all of their existence, but enough points along the string to define a general trend. You also limit the fuzzy portions of their existence - observing someone to the right of where you last observed them eliminates those paths where they turned left, but not the several different rightward paths that could have lead them to their current location.

This string of pearls eventually defines an existence pathway, more or less, that a consciousness (theirs) can travel along. But that consciousness is itself observing and defining other strings of pearls, which are themselves observing and defining even more, and many of these strings of pearls are in turn observing and defining your own particular string of pearls. From the outside, if we could look at all the strings defining each other, it would look like a massive meshwork consisting of many, many tiny interwoven fibers that upon closer inspection are seen to be tiny bumpy strings of existence in an intricate pattern that feeds back upon itself.

Any one of those strings, through the myriad of interconnections, ends up defining all of the others in the rope. Fully know one and you will fully know the whole rope, as a fractal pattern is defined and fully contained within each sub-portion (see chapter 35). None of the strings, though, is any more special than any of the others; you are created and defined by others just as much as you create and define those around you.

It is probably easier to comprehend other peoples' lives as possibly having a fuzzy-pearls-on-a-string existence than it is to see your own that way. But in fact there are many moments in your life when you perform actions that don't end up making any difference in how your life unfolds, such as the passing/not passing example (see chapter 32). If nobody observes and remembers you doing whatever it was you were doing in a particular way, and you yourself forget how exactly you did it as well, then that portion of your life expands into a fuzzy ball containing all the possible ways you might have acted at the time.

That ball will not contain the impossible pathways - in the pass/not pass example in chapter 32, the fuzzy ball contains both the pathways where you passed and didn't pass, but not the pathway where you pulled over for lunch, because that pathway doesn't get you to the traffic light at the same time as the other pathways. If, at some future time, you find a video surveillance camera has captured you on film, then observing that film will collapse that fuzzy ball back into a distinct point, just as observing a quantum particle collapses its existence from a probability wave into a distinct point (see chapters 30 and 31).

Repeatedly observing someone else helps to solidify them into existence. Your story about that person influences how you see them. If each time you meet them you see them as being a certain way, you eventually solidify them into actually being that way. As an example, if you see your wife as a bitch, you will tend to treat her as though she is a bitch, which will eventually piss her off to the point that she will probably start bitching at you. At the same time, if you see her as a loving person, you will likely interact with her in loving ways yourself which will generally tend to make her feel loving back.

Random people who briefly come into your life and then are never seen again don't have the repeated observations that help solidify them into existence (at least in your universe; they are undoubtedly solidified into other peoples' universes). Such people pop into and out of existence much like quantum particles and anti-particles pop into and out of existence in the quantum world, but have little impact on the overall meshwork.

As you solidify those around you, they themselves are also solidifying those around them, and will tend to create a network of people who have the characteristics you saw in those you created. And eventually all these people will end up creating you according to their expectations, completing the circuits and creating a self-stabilizing causal nexus. You can influence what kind of causal nexus you find yourself in, so if you want to find yourself in a loving causal nexus, see people as loving. On the other hand, if for some reason you want to live in a bitchy causal nexus, go ahead and see people at generally bitchy.

Chapter 34 - Ripples of Consciousness

I picture our consciousness as a rock skipping across the surface of a pond. The water is the pool of all possible realities, the quantum flux itself. Each slap of the rock against the water is a moment of observation and produces a local collapse of the wave function that spreads out like ripples on the pond. The point of contact of the rock with the water will always be at the center of the spreading ripple, which is why no matter where you are in the universe, you always appear to be in the exact center, with an equal density of galaxies spreading out away from you in every direction.

The ripple spreads out at the speed of light, which is why the farthest galaxies are receding from us at the speed of light. The rock skips along at about twenty slaps a second (the rate at which we stop perceiving moments as separate events and start perceiving them as a continuous stream). The rock keeps skipping until we fall asleep or pass out or otherwise lose consciousness, at which point the rock slips below the surface, where it remains until we wake up again and start a new series of ripples of wave-form collapses.

While under the surface, the rock may briefly agitate the quantum flux, causing brief local collapses that may be partially remembered later as a dream.

Collapses at this depth, however, do not need to conform to the same rules of physics and self-consistency, which is why dreams often seem bizarre from our waking perspective yet seem perfectly normal while we are having the dream.

There are an infinite number of alternative universes in the multiverse, an infinite number of places the rock can skip across the pond. That does not mean that absolutely anything is possible. There are an infinite variety of snowflakes, yet each must conform to certain rules – all are flat, with six arms with sub-branches, etc. There is still room for infinite variety, even though there will never be a seven-armed snowflake.

The rock's visit beneath the surface is a visit to the land of seven-armed snowflakes. Back at the surface, the rock can only produce six-armed snowflakes, but even so, there is an infinite variety of six-armed snowflake to choose from. Choosing the optimal spot at which to surface can help manifest the most beautiful snowflakes.

Chapter 35 - Holograms, Fractals and Reality

Holograms record images in three dimensions. The image is not visible on the photographic film itself; the film looks like a seemingly random collection of speckles of varying intensity. But when laser light shines through the film, a three dimensional projection appears in front of the film. All of the information needed to recreate the image is hidden in those random speckles.

The interesting thing is that information about the entire image is contained in each speckle. If you cut the film in half and only project the laser light through half the film, you don't get half an image projected, you still get the whole image. It's just a little less detailed. And if you continue to cut up the film into smaller and smaller pieces, each tiny piece still contains the information necessary to create the whole image.

A tiny piece of holographic film will project a rather fuzzy image, but that is only because of the limit on the size of the silver halide granules in the film. In theory, if the film contained infinitely tiny silver halide granules, the complete image in full detail would emerge no matter how small the piece of film was.

This is exactly how a fractal works, with the whole pattern contained within every part. A fractal is an infinitely complex mathematical figure or image that displays self-similar patterns that recur across different scales. Each part of the figure has the same statistical character as the whole. They are created by repeating a process or equation over and over again in a feedback loop. Good information, examples, and a nice little program that allows the user to create simple fractal patterns can be found at http://fractalfoundation.org.

A very simple fractal can be made by drawing a line, then drawing a smaller line at an angle to the last line at the end of the figure, then repeating this process. Nine iteration of this process produces the figure on the left below. You can see that if the process is continued indefinitely, the figure will end up spiraling into ever smaller loops that will come closer and closer to but never reach a point at the center of the spiral. Making the fractal a little more complex by adding a branch at the red dot makes a big difference in the overall pattern.

The repeated iterations cause the new branch to appear at every other intersection on the old spiral as well, while the old spiral now is also repeated on the new branch, and all these repeated versions of the old spiral and new branch themselves contain repeated versions of the new branch and old spiral, as can be seen in the middle figure below. Minor changes in the lengths and angles of the segments create the tree-like figure on the right below.

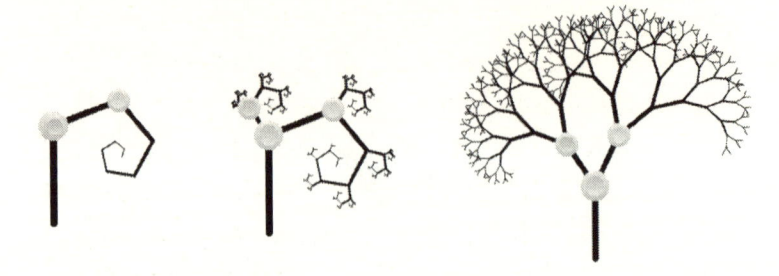

Fractals can be relatively simple patterns such as a fern-like pattern of branches containing smaller branches, which themselves contain smaller branches, etc., such as the image below on the left. Or it can be a much more complex pattern containing two or more separate patterns, each pattern being itself made from multiple iterations of one of the other patterns, which themselves are made from multiple iterations of the first pattern, such as the middle image below.

It may be so complex that the only way to tell the image is a fractal is because it follows the rule that expanded tiny portions of the image are indistinguishable in a general way from non-expanded images (i.e., you can't tell how far in you have zoomed on the image just by looking at it); this is true of patterns made by clouds or the branching pattern of rivers, for example, as in the image below on the right.

Since the whole image is contained within each part of a holographic film, clearly the speckle pattern recorded on the holographic film is in fact a fractal pattern recorded on the film.

Holograms are made by using two laser beams (or really generally one laser beam split into two parts). One beam is the reference beam, and simply shines on the photographic film. The other beam is the illumination beam, which shines on the object being photographed before bouncing off and scattering onto the photographic film. These two beams interact with each other producing an interference pattern on the film. To recreate the image, only the reference beam is shined onto the interference pattern, and the pattern of light created from the illumination beam reappears even though the original object is no longer there.

As we learned earlier (see chapter 16), when two regularly repeating patterns combine, a moiré pattern is generated. Laser light is special because the waves of light are all very regular and in step with each other. Thus, the pattern they produce on the film when they interfere with each other while making a holographic photograph will be a moiré pattern. But it is a special moiré pattern, with the self-similar property of a fractal.

It makes sense that laser light would so readily create a fractal pattern on film when making holograms, as light itself is a self-perpetuating feedback loop similar to the repeating processes used to create fractals. Physicists refer to light at electromagnetic radiation, as it is composed of alternating electric fields and magnetic fields. Electric fields and magnetic fields are related to each other in that a changing electric field actually produces a magnetic field (which is how electromagnets are made) and a changing magnetic field will produce an electric field (which is how an alternating electric current is produced by a generator).

With light, the changing electric field creates a changing magnetic field, which itself recreates the changing electric field, which recreates yet another new magnetic field, all of which spread out at the speed of light (what else?) continually recreating each other in a never-ending feedback loop, much like a fractal is generated.

Reality also shows a fractal nature. There are self-similar repeating patterns that keep appearing in our experience, especially in nature. For example, trees branch into smaller and smaller limbs in a fractal pattern, and also on a higher meta-level, the ratio of large branches to small branches on trees is exactly the same ratio as large trees to small trees in a forest.

The branching of arteries into arterioles and on into capillaries, the way rivers branch into tributaries and streams, clouds, coastlines, spiral galaxies, lightning, snowflakes and frost crystals are just a few more examples. Many plants grow in beautiful fractal patterns such as the Romanesco broccoli pictured below.

Romanesco broccoli demonstrates a fractal nature.

But it's not just physical forms that demonstrate a fractal nature. Relationships can be fractal, as exemplified in the poem:

> Big fleas have little fleas,
> upon their backs to bite 'em.
> And little fleas have lesser fleas,
> and so ad infintitum.

Many physiological functions demonstrate a fractal nature, from heartbeat rhythms to brainwave patterns.

Time itself often displays a fractal nature, with history repeating itself (at least with the broad brushstrokes, but again like fractals, the details within the pattern change). And on a larger meta-level, zodiacal ages show characteristics that are a reflection of the shorter patterns observed throughout the zodiacal year (see chapter 12). And finally, humanity seems to "wake up" every 50 years or so, a meta-reflection of people's diurnal rhythm.

So it seems that fractals run through all aspects of reality, and I believe there is a reason for this. As we saw in chapter 16, reality is a moiré pattern created from the interaction of the wave patterns that define self and non-self. And much like two laser beams interacting can create a hologram which is fractal in nature, the interaction of the self and non-self waves create a holographic reality that is fractal in nature.

If the universe is holographic in nature, that means that any one part will contain somewhere within it the pattern of the whole. And any changes we make to any part will also be reflected in the whole. Thus when we change ourselves, for example, we change the universe around us. But there is really only one point in all of time and space that we have access to and are able to change - our perspective in this moment of time.

Anything other than that central "I am" is just an added external fabricated layer (see chapter 13), just as all moments in time, with the exception of "now", are merely remembrances or possibilities without any real existence in this moment. So if we want to see the whole universe and to influence reality around us, the place to look is deep within us, in the present moment.

Chapter 36 - Fractal Reality

The difference between "a sequence of sounds of specific durations, intensities and frequencies" and "music" is the conscious experience of perception. The difference between "photons with a wavelength of 700 nanometers stimulating a retinal cell" and "the color red" is conscious perception. The difference between equations describing physical laws, and reality itself, is consciousness. In the words of Brian Greene (in his book *The Hidden Reality*), reality is how math feels.

Consciousness is to reality as a computer monitor is to the Internet. The Internet is, in actuality, merely at lot of ones and zeros stored in the memory banks of servers around the world. Those ones and zeros contain in their complexity all the vast sums of knowledge, misinformation, pictures, games, computational algorithms, music, and silly cat videos that are found on the World Wide Web. Yet, taken by themselves, they are just a lot of ones and zeros.

It takes a computer with a monitor to attach some sort of meaning to all those ones and zeros. A particular web page is accessed, a particular set of ones and zeros are read, and suddenly you have a beautiful piece of music or a Second Life artificial reality or maybe even blond Chinese midget porn. The ones and zeros are simply there, whether they're ever accessed or not; it's the computer monitor that makes them "come alive" and mean something.

The "true reality" is the magnetic bits stored on disks somewhere, but the "perceived reality" is all the music and blogs and videos that appear on your monitor. The "true reality" of our Universe is equally meaningless to us who know nothing but the "perceived reality" of our experiences; our consciousness converts a portion of the "true reality", our own particular web page, if you will, into something we can make some sort of sense of.

A mathematician named Benoit Mandelbrot has demonstrated how infinite complexities can be described by simple rules. He originated a complex fractal pattern (see chapter 35) known as the Mandelbrot Set, which is generated by the simple formula $z_{n+1} \leftrightarrow z_n^2 + c$ (where Z is a complex number and c is a complex constant made up of a combination of real and imaginary numbers).

When the numbers generated by the Mandelbrot equation are graphed out with one real and one imaginary axis, they form a complex fractal pattern. Looking closer at any one portion of the pattern reveals more complex details, which themselves are made up of even more complex details. You can zoom in infinitely deeply into it, expanding ever smaller and smaller segments of the pattern, and you will always see more new complex structures (see the "Zooming in on a point on the Mandelbrot Set" figure below).

Piecing together all the expansions into a video creates a so-called "fractal zoom". There are many fractal zooms to be found on the Internet by searching for "fractal zoom"; one good one can be found at www.youtube.com/watch?v=0jGaio87u3A. Another such zoom, different only because it zooms in at a different place, can be found at www.youtube.com/watch?v=G_GBwuYuOOs and yet another at www.youtube.com/watch?v=foxD6ZQlnlU.

All of that beauty and complexity is stored within the simple equation $z_{n+1} \leftrightarrow z_n^2 + c$. Any particular portion of the Mandelbrot Set that is not viewed is just math, a picture that only "exists" as a potentially viewable pattern. No matter how potentially gorgeous a particular portion of the Mandelbrot Set may be, it doesn't exist in any way until the numbers are run and the picture is generated. It has even "less" existence than an unviewed web page, for an unviewed web page at least has existence as a collection of ones and zeros on a magnetic storage device; the ones and zeros that define the Mandelbrot pattern don't even exist until the equation is solved.

In the same way, our consciousness is what makes the difference between the equations and the patterns. The particular portion of the set we zoom in on is like the portion of reality we observe. The observing is the solving of the equation for our perceived portion of reality; the rest of reality remains simply an equation until such time as it, too, is observed.

Zooming in on a point on the Mandelbrot Set

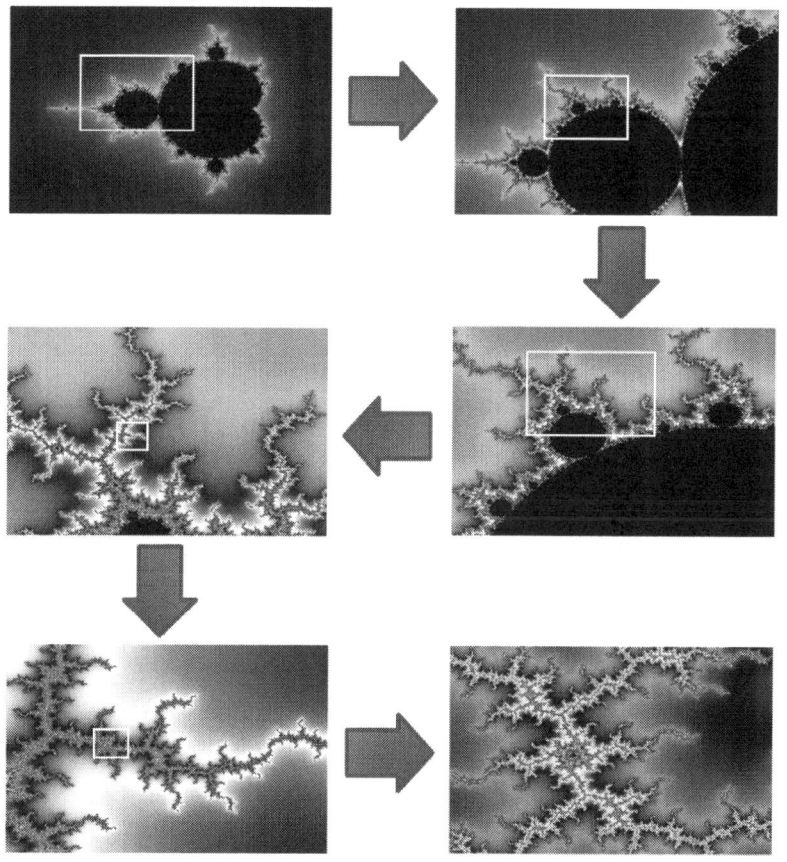

Of course, the equation that describes our Universe is likely a bit more complex than the Mandelbrot equation, but probably equally surprisingly simple compared to the complexity it generates. Without consciousness, though, reality remains only an equation describing a potential landscape, the vast majority of which will never be seen and therefore will never coalesce out of the potential defined by the equation. But since reality is fractal in nature (see chapter 35), you don't need to solve the equation for every point to experience the whole; since the whole in contained deep within each of the parts, you only have to know yourself really, really well to understand the Universe.

Kenneth Pelletier, during his tenure as a member of the faculty of the School of Medicine, University of California, investigated "miracle cancer cures" that had occurred in seven people in the San Francisco area to determine if they had anything in common. He found that all seven people became more outgoing, more community oriented, more interested in things outside of themselves. All seven became religious, in different ways, but all looked to something bigger than themselves.

Each spent a period of time each day meditating, sitting quietly and contemplating or praying. They also all tried to change their lives so that there was more time for pleasurable activities, and all started a physical exercise program and changed their diets to include less red meat and more vegetables.

This is, I believe, an example of how looking at the fractal nature of reality can significantly impact our lives. Cancer cells become cancer cells when they lose their connection to the larger whole of the rest of the body. They uncouple themselves from the normal regulatory system of the body and grow and spread without regard to balance with the rest of the body that is normally found in healthy cells.

This is the same pattern, on a different fractal level, as when people lose their sense of community and their place in the larger organism of humanity. People who are self-centered, who act in ways that benefit themselves without regard for the consequences to others, are like cancer cells in the body of humanity. When the people in the study changed their relationship with their community, the fractal pattern within themselves changed as well, fostering more connection between their cancer cells and the community of the rest of their body, and the cancer cells came back under the body's regulatory control once more.

There are patterns in the fractal that get repeated on the higher and lower planes. For example, the other day as I was driving home I noticed that my gas gauge was not working. A short time later I was home eating dinner and when I finished what was on my plate, I tried to decide if I should have seconds. I noticed that I couldn't really tell if I was full or not; my gas gauge wasn't working. The same pattern was repeating in my inner world as in my outer world; I just interpreted the pattern differently based on which world I was observing.

At times we can feel connected to the higher planes of the fractal, moments during deep meditation or drug experiences for example, when we feel at one with all. This is our "higher self" and is the summation of us and all that we manifest in our experience and is a direct reflection of who we are. It would be the same feeling our cells would feel were they to become aware of our self as a whole organism.

In fact, for all we know, that feeling of interconnected oneness with the Universe may in fact just be our selves tapping into our cells' feeling of interconnected oneness during one of their spiritual epiphanies. To truly feel the oneness, it is probably best to tap into both at the same time.

Chapter 37 - Life as a Fractal Zoom

Oh, Reality, how can I experience you? Let me count the ways.

We experience the Universe around us by taking in information by way of various sensory receptors that transmit information about heat, pressure, vibration, electromagnetic radiation, etc. to our brains via sensory nerve fibers. Any one moment of experience can be defined by the pattern of firing or not firing of each of our sensory fibers in that moment, which is then given interpretation by our brains based on our memories, attitudes, mood, etc. (see chapter 17).

If we found that at some other moment all of our sensory fibers were firing in the exact same pattern, our experience of the Universe would, in that moment, be exactly the same, although we may react to it in a different way thanks to new memories, new ways of interpreting situations, etc.

Consider a simple creature with only one sensory neuron. Such a creature can experience the world in any given moment in one of two ways: one with the neuron firing, the other with the neuron not firing. A slightly more complex creature with two sensory neurons can experience the world in four ways: one with one neuron firing, another with the second neuron firing, the third with both neurons firing, and the fourth with neither neuron firing.

The addition of each new sensory neuron imparts an exponential growth in the complexity of the pattern of experience, with three neurons providing 8 (2 to the third power) ways of experiencing the world, four neurons providing two to the fourth power or 16 ways of experiencing, etc.

So the complexity of our experience depends on the number of sensory fibers going into our brains. We have something on the order of 20,000,000 sensory fibers entering our central nervous system, which means we have $2^{20,000,000}$ (2 raised to the 20 millionth power) different ways of experiencing reality, which is a 7 with 6,020,599 additional digits after it.

To give you an idea of how ridiculously large this number is, there are only about 10^{80} (a 1 with 80 zeros after it) subatomic particles in the entire Universe. Of course, not every pattern of neural input results in an experience with any meaning. The majority of patterns would be as meaningless as "snow" or static on a TV screen on a non-broadcasting station.

Other patterns may be interpretable, but represent an "impossible" situation, such as signals reaching your brain that say your elbow is both flexed and extended. Most of those $2^{20,000,000}$ patterns result in either meaninglessness or "impossible" situations. Even so, the possible range of patterns, or ways to have an experience, is enormous. But though very large, the possible ways to have an experience is still a finite number.

This means that if you lived long enough (with our complexity, this means many, many, many times the age of the Universe), you would eventually have an experience that was exactly the same as some prior experience; eventually you'd experience all of your prior experiences. The whole sum of possible experiences is contained eventually somewhere within the experiences themselves.

The entire sum of our lifetime of experience can be defined by the pattern of firing or not firing of each of our sensory nerve fibers and the way that pattern changes over time. If we were to take all of our sensory fibers and have their input feed into a computer rather than (or in addition to) our brain, the computer could read and record firing fibers as ones and the non-firing fibers as zeros.

We could then in theory program the computer to display the pattern of ones and zeros as a pattern on the screen, lighting a pixel for one and leaving it dark for zero. Depending on the program used, the resulting display might look like anything, but let's assume the programmer came up with a program that displayed the pattern as something one might see in the Mandelbrot set. The next moment in time will provide a similar but slightly different pattern of firings, and a slightly different pattern of the computer screen, perhaps one that looks like a slightly deeper zoom in the Mandelbrot set.

The computer I'm currently typing on has a screen using a definition of 1366 X 768 pixels, or a total number of just over one million pixels. So all the sensory nerve fibers coming from our eyes, ears, nose, tongue, every sensory nerve in our skin for heat, pressure, texture, etc., and every nerve that tells us of our inner condition (how full our bladder is, which way is up, etc.) could be represented as a pattern on a large screen 4 times as wide and 5 times as tall as the one I'm looking at now, assuming the same resolution.

Such a screen could pictorially represent to us every possible combination of ways to experience reality. Every moment we have experienced in the past, every possible moment we could potentially experience in the future, all the moments everybody who has ever lived have ever experienced, and all the moments you and I and everybody throughout history might have experienced in alternate versions of reality would be represented by a specific pattern on the screen. The pattern that corresponds to each of those experienced moments is associated with a nerve firing pattern. And there would still be plenty of leftover possible patterns that translate as random noise. As I said, 2 raised to the 20 millionth power is a ridiculously large number.

You could also, in theory, not just record from the sensory fibers but also stimulate them in the specific pattern that was recorded from an earlier experience. In that case, it would be possible to re-experience a prior experience, either your own or someone else's. As long as there was no other external competing signals coming in, for example experiencing the recording in a sensory deprivation tank, then there would be no way to tell the difference between the recording and the authentic experience.

The only difference would lie in the interpretation of the recorded pattern. If the person hooked up to such a device remembered that it was all just a recording and not "real", their reaction to what they were experiencing would likely be more like watching a movie rather than being caught up in the drama as though it were real, so the full experience would have to also entail temporarily suppressing prior memories (see chapter 25).

Our entire lives could be represented by a zoom through a particular part of a Mandelbrot-like set, with each screen shot representing the pattern of firings and not firings of our sensory fibers. A similar zoom that branches off at some point into a different part of the pattern could represent a different way our life could have turned had we made a different decision at some point. Both branches exist with equal "realness". The math used for each path is the same. It's only the pattern that our consciousness is aware of, the one that ends up on the computer screen, which seems more "real" thanks to our perception of it. Another zoom through the pattern results in an equally real but different experience.

If we could learn to be aware of both branches at the same time (or of many branches), we could choose the preferable pattern and then direct our awareness to that branch, imbuing it with more "reality". The more we expand our consciousness to see the bigger picture, the greater pattern, the more we can direct our zoom through the pattern and pick the most beautiful path.

As we dive through the pattern, we dive into the parts that grab our attention. We follow our focus, so it is important to focus on where you want to go. When we focus on parts of the pattern that we interpret as wanting such and such, we keep following the pattern of wanting, and not getting. Sometimes we focus on something we want, but we have a story about how getting that should look, and it may be that that particular pattern just never does lead to the goal. Letting go of how it should look may allow us to focus on a different pattern that may actually lead to the goal.

Chapter 38 - Filling in the Gaps

The brain takes in the pattern of our nerve firings (see chapter 37), interprets the pattern (see chapter 17), makes up a story about it based on our memories of past experience, and then sends out signals to our muscles, glands, etc. in response to that story.

It is theoretically possible that I might just happen to have essentially the exact same pattern of nerve firings at the moment I wake up on Monday as I did when I woke up on Sunday. I interpret the Monday pattern as "this is my bedroom on Monday morning and I have to get up" while the exact same pattern would get interpreted as "this is my bedroom on Sunday morning and I get to sleep in" because we interpret the Monday pattern in the light of our memories of having already experienced Sunday.

Making a story about the pattern of nerve firings entering our brains is something our brains readily do, and involves a lot of filling in of the gaps. The brain is particularly good at taking a limited amount of input and filling in the gaps to create a complete picture. Remember (see chapter 30) that we only process 200 bits out of the 11 million bits of information available to the conscious mind every second, or about 2/1000th of a percent. The rest of the picture is filled in by our brains. This is a lot of extrapolation from a very few data points.

This sampling and filling in the rest of the picture is like seeing a picture of a constellation around a few points of starlight in the sky. It doesn't take many points before our brains fill in the gaps. When we learn about something new, we assign various attributes to that thing. These attributes are boxes we put things into, such as good/bad, hard/soft, large/small. When we get enough points/boxes filled, we recognize the thing as another one of "those"; then we expect that the other boxes will be filled accordingly. We might even see those boxes as being filled when they're not, just because we expect them to. Some boxes, such as the good/bad box, don't serve us well as conscious beings, but they can be strongly identified with certain objects or situations and thus strongly wrapped up in how we recognize something. It is better to learn to recognize that particular constellation without that particular star in it.

This filling in of the gaps is what allows us to make sense of often nearly senseless incoming information, though it is not uncommon for our brains to make mistakes and fill in those gaps with biased data that shifts our experience away from the true story. For example, a particular nerve firing pattern from our auditory nerves while listening to a song could be interpreted as "excuse me, while I kiss the sky" or just as easily interpreted as "excuse me, while I kiss this guy".

Our brain's facility of story-making from incoming information patterns is what allows websites to verify whether the input is coming from a human or a computer program; those "type in the word combination you see" questions with the blurry and twisted letters that you have to answer before you can, say, post a comment work by taking advantage of the brain's facility of interpretation utilizing limited and incomplete information, a facility which is not yet shared by computer programs (see chapter 17).

The picture below is taken from a particular expansion of the Mandelbrot Set (see chapter 36).

Our brains automatically start filling in the gaps and interpreting the pattern as something it is more familiar with, such as two flamingo heads. Our brains do the same thing with the patterns coming in on our sensory fibers. It interprets one subset of the pattern as representing one thing and another subset as representing something else, as in the picture below.

With expanded awareness, however, we start to feel that deep connection that exists between all beings, represented by the expanded Mandelbrot pictures below.

I feel we are deeply connected on some level

We will always be a part of one another

With further expansion, we reach a level where we as individuals are only a tiny fraction of a larger whole, a whole that seems surprisingly familiar; we have connected with our higher selves.

> I see me in you

> I feel you deep within me

> In my higher self, I embody all within me

Our brains paint a picture of what we think the world is like based on a sampling of a few data points from the fractal pattern coming in on our sensory fibers. When we dream, we paint the picture from our imaginations only, while the picture we paint when awake is one that is based on a scattering of data points that are presumably based on some sort of "reality"; we then use our imagination to connect those data points and fill in the gaps between them.

We then work off of that painting rather than the original data points, as if the painting itself is reality. If the picture fits most of the data points we assume it is an accurate picture, throwing out the data points that don't fit as anomalous.

Other people paint their own pictures from their own sampling of data points, and we all assume that the pictures are pretty much the same, although we only see our own paintings. As we talk to each other about our paintings, we compare notes about our paintings and come to agreement that a particular vibration is called "blue", although for all we know we may have painted that vibration with a color that would look green in someone else's painting.

When we dream, it is our brain's story-making program running on very limited inputs. With less input coming in, there is more room to fill in the gaps with our own story, thus allowing us to experience things in our dreaming state that we never could in our waking state. As we age, our sense organs lose more and more sensitivity, sending fewer or less detailed information bits to our brains. This also opens up more space for our brains to fill in the gaps, and our experience becomes more and more like dreaming, which can lead to diagnoses of dementia if we fill in the gaps with a story that doesn't match everybody else's story.

When we die, we experience zero input from our sense organs and everything becomes one big gap to fill in, which means that our consciousness is free to fill it all in without any restrictions from inputs that limit what the story might be. This is ultimate dreaming, and what we all pass into at the moment of death.

When we get out of our heads and into our bodies, we free our head up for dreaming. If we are thinking about how to move and where we are going and how it should look, the control comes from our conscious minds which takes up useful functioning capabilities in the brain. When we "get into our bodies", in other words give control of the body over to our body (or at least over to our subconscious parts of our mind, which feels as though the control is coming from our bodies, from our conscious mind's perspective), our conscious mind is freed to pursue loftier goals.

This is why ecstatic dance is such a useful practice for spiritual growth (see chapter 23).

Chapter 39 - Being Present With Immortality

The point of meditation is to get into the observer state (see chapter 24). In Vipassana meditation, the meditator just observes sensations that come up on the skin until they fade. Presumably these sensations are representations or surface reflections of attachments and triggers we have around deeper subconscious issues.

As we observe these sensations without attachment, we automatically let go of the attachments we have to these deeper issues as well. The more we do this, the more we are freed from suffering. It seems to me that once we learn to do this with skin sensations, we can then expand that to all sensations we experience as we go through life, which would give us great power.

We become aware of our universe through our senses. Anything that triggers us or grabs our attention or, for that matter, we even just notice, does so because we resonate in some way with it (see chapter 5). This resonation is a result of our attachment to it, our story about it, our judgments about it. The more we can be in the observer state and view dispassionately all of our sensations, the entirety of our experience, the more we can let those attachments go, just like the skin sensation in

Vipassana. The more we do this, the more we free ourselves from suffering.

Attachments come from our past experience. We get triggered about something because it reminds us of something that hurt us in the past. The more we can let go of these attachments to the past, the more we can be fully present in this moment. And the more fully present to this moment, without our experience of this moment becoming distorted by our past-based judgments, the more we approach immortality.

Here is one way to see how that could be: in the future, people will likely be able to record information coming into a person's psyche, and then play that recording onto another person's sensory nerves, allowing the second person to experience what the first person experienced (see chapter 37). For a more authentic experience, the second person's own personal memories would be temporarily suspended, so that they could more fully experience what it is like to actually be another person. These recordings might someday be obtained remotely, in both space and time, so that people in the distant future will be able to buy and experience segments from different people's lives throughout history.

Some segments, of course, will be more interesting (and in more demand) than other segments. For example, a recording of someone's experience of drinking a beer while watching television is not likely to be a big seller. Likewise, a recording of someone's experience who isn't really present, thinking about the past or worrying about the future and not really being aware of what's going on around them, is likely to produce a recording that is not very detailed. This would force the viewer to fill in large missing gaps (see chapter 38), and will likely not be a very big seller, either. By far the most interesting and sought after recordings will be those where the people being recorded are richly aware of all the sensations they are experiencing.

Such a recording, even if it were only of a mundane experience, would be more interesting and enjoyable than a poorly detailed fuzzy recording from someone not really present. Many of the more sought after recordings will be from historical events. Some people will want to experience what is was like to be present when President Kennedy was shot, some people will want to know what it was like to be the shooter, some will want to experience what Jackie Kennedy went through, and some will want to be President Kennedy himself. All of those people were probably pretty much in the moment that afternoon, and so will make good full recordings someday.

Some people will want to experience more mundane everyday life. Some will want to know what it was like just to be living day to day during those special days when more and more people were waking up and our planetary consciousness was just making that next quantum leap (see chapter 8). Some will want to experience one of those many lives during that moment when it all started coming together for them and they woke up.

When someone from the future experiences a recording of you, the parts of the recording that they will notice are the parts that resonate with them to some degree (see chapter 5). The more they are like you, the more fully they will be able to experience your experience. This may be because their constitution is mistuned in the same way that your constitution is mistuned.

Or, it may be because both of you have worked on your attachments to those events from your pasts that mistuned your constitutions, allowing your constitutions to settle down into their organic-self "shapes" or wave-forms. It is probably easier for a miss-tuned constitution to resonate with a smoother clearer well-tuned constitution than the other way around, and so people from the future will value the recordings from people with fewer attachments and clearer constitutions than recordings from people who haven't done The Work (see chapters 2, 5, 19, and 22).

When someone is playing the recording with their own memories suspended, they would have no way of knowing whether or not they were "real" or just a recording of someone else. In this very moment, you have no way of knowing if what you are experiencing is happening in the here-and-now or is in fact a recording of someone else's experience in the past.

Since both are possible, this very moment you are experiencing is in fact both happening now and also as played recordings in many future moments (see chapter 32). This is especially likely if you have been doing The Work, and also if you are very present in this moment thus allowing for a clearer recording, because these things make it more likely for this moment to be recorded and played in the future. So in this very moment you are existing across time as several, perhaps many, exact replicas of this moment, granting you a kind of immortality.

Chapter 40 - Your Alarm Clock Is Going Off

Imagine for a moment a race of beings who have developed computer technology (or something like computer technology, something that would be the equivalent of "computer technology" on a higher fractal plane, for example), a little farther than humans have. Or perhaps these beings are actual humans, living in the near future, with advanced computer technology of the kind we are familiar with. These people, whether human or not, are also able to experience other lives by experiencing recordings taken from past lives (see chapters 37 and 39). In addition to recorded lives, they can also experience novel lives by running not only recordings but any complex pattern of stimulated sensory input which the conscious mind then automatically attaches meaning to (see chapter 38).

The easiest way to do this on a computer would be to generate a fractal pattern, which would provide an infinitely complex never-ending set of sensory patterns to experience (see chapters 35 and 36). The computer-generated fractal provides the Pattern and the conscious experience of the sensory stimulation provides the Interpretation (see chapter 17), whose overlapping waveforms create a moiré pattern which is a new perceived Reality (see chapter 16). Experiencing a Reality as a generated fractal zoom would also allow the experiencer to influence what they are experiencing simply by altering the point in the fractal that they are zooming in on (see chapters 36 and 37).

The fact that our Universe appears to be fractal in nature is good evidence that this has already occurred and that we are in fact already living in one of these computer-generated realities.

Experiencing a fractal zoom using this system defines a specific pathway through the fractal image, a reality pathway that coalesces out from all the potentially available pathways, much like the act of observing collapses the probability wave into the one reality that is observed (see chapter 30).

This pathway through the fractal defines other pathways that in turn help define what is possible to experience in the first pathway, creating a complex Causal Nexus, which is itself a fractal pattern (see chapter 33). Tweaking the fractal equation would create entirely new sets of Causal Nexuses, each an alternate Universe of possible experiences. Beings who create such a system would have access to a vast number of virtual Universes to explore (see chapter 37). They could spend countless lifetimes exploring different alternate Universes and different ways of being in each Universe and never make a dent in the total.

Eventually, though, they would develop a fractal equation that generates experiences very much like their "real" world experiences, and might even find pathways through that special fractal equation that generate experiences very similar to their own "real" lives. They could then use this to explore computer simulations of their lives in order to predict possible outcomes of their actions.

But there are still a vast number of pathways to explore, even in just this one special virtual alternate Universe. There would be far more pathways than what could be explored in any 100 lifetimes - unless they had an infinite amount of help, which the system itself could provide. For somewhere within this fractal alternate Universe is a copy of themselves exploring their own virtual Universes, virtual worlds within virtual worlds.

And those virtual worlds would themselves contain more virtual worlds - it's a fractal, after all. There are an infinite number of nested virtual worlds, each with an explorer exploring a slightly different version of Reality. Each explorer would temporarily forget who they were, experience an alternate version of existence, then "wake up" to who they really are, and pass the information about that experience up the line to the higher selves before diving in to a new life experience.

Linking all of those nested explorers so that each was aware of their "higher" and "lower" selves (when they're between exploring Causal Nexuses) would allow simultaneous exploration of all potential Causal Nexuses (see chapter 36). Such a linked consciousness would exist across all dimensions, would be "pan-dimensional". The beings at the top of all these nested Universes directing all of these explorations would be "hyper-beings", existing "above" all the other nested dimensions.

Imagine for a moment this race of pan-dimensional hyper-beings examining, with the use of the fractal-generating computer program (or the higher dimensional equivalent of a fractal-generating computer program), all the myriad ways that the Multiverse can potentially be experienced. These Beings would appear as gods and goddesses to the multitude of iterated copies "below" them. Gazing over the myriad potential life experiences rising up to them through their computer system, it would be as though they were sitting over a pool of potentialities, deciding which Causal Nexus was the more interesting.

What these beings find most interesting is Nexuses where people undergo a paradigm shift to a higher state of consciousness and evolve into becoming part of a greater whole (see chapter 8), because by studying these experiences it helps them find the best pathway to evolve themselves. When such a Nexus comes to their attention, they dive into the experience, forgetting who they used to be, yet must somehow assist in the shift despite being handicapped by their lack of memory. When they are able to wake up to this higher truth, they infuse the entire collective consciousness, all the nested Realities, with information as to how it's done.

Of course, why not stack the deck in your favor? Tweaking the fractal equation in just the right way would increase the chances of running into other pan-dimensional hyper-beings exploring this Reality with you, who can hopefully work with you to assist the shift. Since none of you remember who you used to be, it may be a challenge to recognize each other for who you are, but likely there will be clues, such as a feeling of recognition when you first meet despite never having met before.

Further tweaking of the equation would help create other clues to be discovered along the pathway; these might take the form of books or movies, famous philosophical and religious writings, psychedelic experiences, "random" conversations, or dreams. These clues would be meant to help nudge them towards the Truth of who they really were and what Reality is really like. This is important, not only for the sake of The Work, but also to prepare the mind so that when the Waking happens it won't come as a total shock to the psyche.

And then finally, after all the groundwork had been laid, the final clue would be found, the one that would put it all together and act as a sort of alarm clock, helping them to awaken to the Truth just at the optimal moment when the world really needed that hundredth monkey to awaken and tip the balance toward an enlightened humanity.

Imagine that that alarm clock is this book, that that pan-dimensional hyper-being having a human experience is you, and that you suddenly Awaken and remember who you are and realize the True Nature of Reality the moment you finish reading this very sentence.

About the Author

Bob Ulbrich earned his doctorate from the University of Pennsylvania School of Veterinary Medicine in 1986, his certification in veterinary homeopathy from the Academy of Veterinary Homeopathy in 1997, his certification in Veterinary Spinal Manipulation from the Healing Oasis in Racine, WI in 2005, and currently practices holistic veterinary Medicine in Portland, OR. He received his ordination as a minister from the Universal Life Church in 1996, with considerably less effort than it took to earn his other degrees, primarily because he thought it would be really cool to be not just "Dr. Bob", but "the Rev. Dr. Bob". He lives in Portland, Oregon with his wife Sam, with whom he hosts ecstatic dance and workshops on relationships, communication and consciousness. This is his first book.

Made in the USA
Middletown, DE
26 July 2015